TWO FACES OF JANUS

TWO FACES OF JANUS

The Saga of Deep South Change

J. OLIVER EMMERICH

UNIVERSITY AND COLLEGE PRESS
OF MISSISSIPPI

JACKSON

1973

Copyright © 1973 by
The University and College Press of Mississippi
Library of Congress Catalog Card Number 72-94351
ISBN Number 0-87805-017-5
Manufactured in the United States of America
Printed by Benson Printing Company, Nashville, Tenn.
Designed by J. Barney McKee

To Lyda Will
Who never grows weary of well doing

Acknowledgments

ANYONE ATTEMPTING to assemble a diversity of facts, by the very nature of the situation, finds himself indebted to many individuals and institutions, so many so that it is impractical to name them all. Nevertheless, I particularly want to thank the Mississippi Library Commission, the State Department of Archives and History, the Library of Congress, the personnel of my own hometown library, many dedicated authors whose resource material made this story possible, Mrs. Audrey Thomas, my research assistant, and Mrs. Billie Kavanay, my efficient secretary. To all who helped I am very grateful.

Foreword

THIS STORY OF the Deep South that was and the Deep South that is reveals an enormous contrast, the extent of which most Americans do not, as yet, realize.

Nine thousand students at Mississippi State University balloted to determine who would be "Mr. MSU" of 1972. When the votes were counted on this predominantly white campus, Frank Dowsing, a black senior, a pre-med student, and the All-American defense safety, received the coveted honor.

In October, 1972, a class of licensed practical nurses was graduated from Southwest Mississippi Junior College. In keeping with tradition, members of the class balloted to determine the "class favorite," an honor based upon an individual's personality and contribution. Edward Russ, a black student, was named.

For forty years the community of McComb, Mississippi, through the leadership of its hometown newspaper, has chosen a "Mother of the Year," an honor reflecting the highest qualities of motherhood. In May, 1972, the selection committee chose Mrs. Sidney Nash—a black mother—not because she was black, but because she had exhibited the highest qualities of motherhood in rearing and educating her eight children. Instances such as those mentioned here have happened throughout the Deep South in recent years.

FOREWORD

The selection of black persons as "Mr. MSU," "class favorite," and "Mother of the Year" did not result from court orders, federal funds, or boycotts. Instead, new dimensions of change have appeared in the Deep South, the dimensions of good will and understanding.

The Roman Janus, mythological god of doorways and archways, has been portrayed throughout history with two faces, each looking in a different direction. In this book, King Cotton is given the two faces of Janus, not because he looks in two directions, but because as the embodiment of saint and sinner he requires the faces of both. The two faces of Janus appearing in the South are not, however, restricted to King Cotton. Others include the Janus of race, black and white; the Janus of heritage, freedom and slavery; the Janus of the Deep South historically, one face looking back to the past and the other looking forward to the future.

This book explores the philosophy of backwardness which evolved throughout the years and the part the spirit of Janus played in its development. Although the traditions of yesteryear have continued to influence the Deep South during the twentieth century, the miracle is the Deep South change—a transformation in will, understanding, and regional behavior which has occurred with an amazing quickening of tempo—a miracle which millions of Americans do not as yet realize has happened.

Life in the Deep South was dominated by the cotton economy and its accompanying aspects. Throughout the world, the history of cotton regions has been by no means tranquil. The cotton culture aroused sectional hostilities

FOREWORD

and caused people of the Deep South to believe that everyone outside the region was opposed to them. Rather than critically analyzing the situation, they became emotional and demanded conformity to the system. Because of cotton's drain on the soil, the one-crop economy degenerated into a poverty-perpetuating system for the masses. Then suddenly, when the philosophy took on new dimensions, the speed of its change was almost a miracle.

Throughout the years, both editorially and in speeches to various clubs and conventions, I have sought to encourage citizens in the Deep South to enter the mainstream of American life. I must confess, however, if you are a Deep South southerner you're caught up in a snare. You try to lead people out, only to realize you are a part of the thing you lament. You discover, to your own amazement, that you have somehow accepted the prejudices you oppose. I don't mean that you do this deliberately—acceptance is a part of your inheritance. It happens unknowingly. It creeps into your blood stream, so to speak. You sense an evil in sectional prejudices, and something reminds you day by day that this cotton philosophy is one of backwardness. If your people, your neighbors, your friends, your region, are to reach for greatness, a change must be made in the philosophy which determines the direction in which the people will move.

No one wants to be a nobody. Everyone seeks a feeling of well-being—the essence of human dignity, of knowing he is somebody. The point was well illustrated when a contest was held to determine the "best teacher in the United States." The judges' selection, so it was said, was

FOREWORD

influenced by a letter from an eleven-year-old pupil of the winner, a teacher from Jackson, Mississippi. The student wrote, "My teacher is the best teacher in the world because she makes me feel like I'm somebody."

The sharing of human dignity requires no expenditure of money. It can come only from the heart. During recent years, an acknowledgment of the human dignity inherent in the members of all races has spread rapidly throughout the Deep South. Suddenly, almost overnight, residents of the South have recognized the elemental truth expressed by the young boy in the letter praising his teacher.

Contents

    Acknowledgements vi
    Foreword vii
1 More Cursed Than Blessed 3
2 Three Unforgettable Characters 19
3 Lesson in Retrospect 29
4 The Dipping Vat War 34
5 High Cost of Demagoguery 44
6 Russian Roulette 55
7 Fetter in Washington 72
8 States' Rights Campaign 87
9 Outside the Mainstream of America 104
10 Soul Searching 108
11 "Go to Jail First" 119
12 Reign of Terror 131
13 The Sheriff's Request 143
14 The Road to Damascus 151
    Index 159

TWO FACES OF JANUS

More Cursed Than Blessed

WHEN NUMA POMPILIUS devised his calendar, he named the first month in honor of Janus, the mythical god of gates and doors, the keeper of heaven and earth. As doors lead in as well as out, Janus was portrayed with two faces, each commanding a view of a different direction.

King Cotton, whose realm includes sixty nations where his crop is cultivated, cannot be restricted to Roman or Grecian mythology. His domain is world-wide in scope. Sometimes he is king, sometimes renegade. But as he is consistently schizophrenic, he is well qualified to be portrayed with two faces, not as the keeper of heaven and earth as was the case with Janus, but as the miasmal promoter of heaven and hell.

There is far more reality than fancy in this characterization of King Cotton. To perceive the full meaning of this fable is to comprehend the complexities of the Deep South and to understand the pattern of both the southern conscience and the southern mind. Without an understanding of the double faces of the Cotton Janus it is difficult—if not impossible—for one to comprehend the revolutionary meaning of what is happening today in the South in the twentieth century.

In the United States—and the South in particular—cotton has been both a blessing and a curse, but more curse, by far, than blessing. The most sinister curse which cotton has bequeathed to the Deep South is what I choose to call a "cotton patch" philosophy—a philosophy of backwardness.

In the twenties, before I launched into a newspaper career, I served as a county farm agent with the Mississippi Agricultural Extension Service. I had majored in agriculture at what is now Mississippi State University and at the University of Missouri.

In that day the personnel of agricultural experiment stations were busily engaged in finding ways to control plant diseases, to develop new and more profitable varieties of crops, to establish improved methods of cultivation, and to determine the most effective methods of soil improvement and crop diversification. But the one-crop, poverty-perpetuating cotton economy had such a hold on the people that few responded to new ideas and new discoveries.

Most farmers resisted anything in any way related to change. Scientific agriculture was laughed aside as book farming. I have had farmers say to me, "My pa did it this way and if it was good enough for him it is good enough for me." Often farmers spoke of their farm experience in terms of how many farms they had worn out.

Thousands of emaciated, pallid-faced, listless, barefooted children were infested with hookworms. The state board of health made an earnest effort to cope with this and similar maladies. The cotton-patch philosophy was well expressed by a woman who said, "I'm not going to let any one of those out-of-town nurses tell me what to do with my own children." Seeking to reassure her I said, "But they may help your children. That's their reason for being here." But she doggedly held to her position. "I don't care," she replied. "I'm not letting any outsiders tell me what to do with my own children."

The average farmer looked to the furnishing merchant for his flour and fertilizer, his coffee and tobacco, paid high interest for being "furnished," deplored the boll weevil, lamented the high cost of school books, and at the end of the year, after sharing his crop with his landowner or paying the interest on his mortgage, did well if he was able to buy a Sunday suit or even an extra pair of overalls.

The system was such that the poor grew poorer and the rich richer, but even at that, the number of well-to-do folk was limited. I can recall the day when I could count on my fingers the men who came to town from over the county on Saturdays wearing a coat and tie. The others wore their usual work clothes, a fact which reflected the poverty created by the one-crop cotton economy.

Cotton is merely a plant, a cousin of the elegant hibiscus, a perennial which in its natural, tropical habitat, grows fifteen feet tall. To comprehend the effect of this intriguing plant upon the people of the Deep South and to perceive how an entire region could be tied to a philosophy of backwardness because of it, one must review its history. Worldwide, this history includes thousands of years; but from the viewpoint of this region, it is limited to a century and a half.

Cotton's diversified history is reflected in both time and

geography. It was grown in the Indus Valley, now a part of Pakistan, nearly as long ago as 3,000 B.C.[1]* The Egyptian pharaohs were acquainted with it. The oldest cotton textiles were used about five thousand years ago. Mummies wrapped in cotton cloth have been found in Peru. The cotton cloth found there has been verified to be at least 4,500 years old. Cortez, marching across the New World, reported that the Aztecs were skilled artisans in the spinning and weaving of cotton.[2]

When the new republic of the United States of America was launched following the revolutionary struggle, it sorely needed to export goods to other countries of the world in order to grow strong economically. Cotton, the psychotic Janus, abundantly blessed the budding young nation. After the invention of the cotton gin, cotton provided the economic stability to bolster the economy and made it possible to develop a balance-of-payments structure which served as the credentials for growing international respect, as well as a subtle appreciation of the young nation's power to defend itself.[3]

The story of Widow Nathanael Green's invitation to Eli Whitney to visit her Georgia plantation on the Savannah River shortly after the young mechanical genius was graduated from Yale is as familiar to most Americans as George Washington's crossing the Delaware River. Responding to the urgent appeal of a group of southern cotton planters, Whitney applied his talents to the task of developing a machine which would separate cotton seed from the lint that entwined it.[4]

* Notes appear at end of chapter.

MORE CURSED THAN BLESSED

This machine of empire-building proportions became more significant after Matthew Boulton and James Watts built a factory at Soho, near Birmingham, England, to manufacture steam engines for general use.[5] A few years before, Watts had invented the steam engine and now a manufacturing plant was to be established which would enable textile machines to be powered by steam. Still further revolutionary events occurred when much larger, faster, and more versatile textile machines were developed almost simultaneously with the steam engines to power them.

Three epoch-making events had converged in a moment in history to open doors to new horizons. England's capacity to manufacture textiles had doubled, tripled, quadrupled—and the world increasingly needed cotton fabrics. But to manufacture textiles the British had to have raw cotton—much of it—and the young American nation was ready to capitalize upon an expanded market for a raw material she could produce.

Cotton requires a reasonably fertile soil, an abundance of sunshine, a two-hundred-frost-free-days growing season, and the labor to cultivate the crop in the spring and to harvest it in the autumn.[6] The South had the land, the sunshine, and the growing season. The labor was available through the African slave markets. It was almost as if man and nature had formed a conspiracy to grow cotton. At this juncture in history, Janus, this mythical figure, stood ready both to bless and to curse the nation.

The cotton monarch flexed his muscles. From 1793, the year of Whitney's invention, to 1800, cotton production in the United States increased from 3,000 bales to 70,000. These were the days of swaddling clothes for the southern cotton realm. By 1815 production had soared to 150,000 bales. In the five years between 1815 and 1820 production doubled. It had doubled again by 1826 and again between 1830 and 1837. By 1851, the crop was twice the size of that produced in 1837. By 1859, it was double that of 1849. By 1859, the South's cotton production had reached 4,500,000 bales.[7]

By 1851, cotton constituted 40 percent of the nation's total exports. The cotton Janus was then a saint. By 1857, total exports of the country had reached a value of $340,000,000, one half of which was attributable to cotton. The value of cotton exports reached $191,806,000 by 1860.[8]

Cotton production in the South is not measured from time immemorial. In *The Mind of the South*, W. J. Cash wrote, "From 1820 to 1860 is but 40 years—a little more than the span of one generation. The whole period from the invention of the cotton gin to the outbreak of the Civil War is less than 70 years—the lifetime of a single man. Yet, it was wholly in this longer period and mainly in the shorter that the development of the Cotton South took place."

King Cotton by this time had ascended the throne in the Southland. The stars and stripes of Old Glory were bulwarked by the strength of cotton fibre. Cotton had blessed America.

As the production of cotton climbed to 4,500,000 bales by 1859, it was matched by an equally staggering expansion in the number of slaves owned by southern planters.[9]

Between the time of the invention of Whitney's gin and the eve of the War Between the States in 1860, the number of slaves owned in the South increased from 700,000 to 4,300,000.[10] Janus the saint had become Janus the sinner.

The prodigious number of slaves imported into the South during the boom days of cotton was by no means the full extent of this regional and national tragedy. Even in the early period of this cotton aggression—during the administrations of Presidents James Monroe and John Quincy Adams—slavery was becoming less acceptable in the South. History records that slavery was "on its way out in the South." There were more anti-slavery societies in the slave states than there were in the free states. "The South," David Cohn wrote, "was looking squarely at the evils of slavery."

This fact was demonstrated by a debate in the Virginia Assembly on the subject of "Emancipation." The debate in the legislature was part of an effort to free the slaves in Virginia. The effort to abolish slavery did not succeed; but, nonetheless, slavery had been condemned in the Virginia Assembly by legislative representatives of a slaveholding people.[11] The brutal demands of the Cotton Janus, however, changed all this. Within a few years, scarcely a voice was to be lifted in the South in defense of emancipation. The face turned. By 1837, there was not one anti-slavery society in the South.[12]

As slavery increased and the cotton business expanded, loyalty to the South came to mean conformity to what would best promote cotton. Conformity was a part of the philosophy of backwardness. The institution which for a period had been blamed for the ills of the region was now held forth as the basis for its superiority and the reason for its fancied perfection.

This reversal of the southern trend—this turning away from the potential goal of emancipation in the South—was historically catastrophic. What it did to the white people of the South, as well as to the blacks, was a human cataclysm.

While the South was experiencing this cogent growth in plantation output, the mythical King Cotton was promoting "heaven and hell" in England and other parts of the world. For centuries England had been a major producer of woolen goods. English herdsmen raised sheep; English textile operators were in the majority and possessed greater political influence than the cotton weavers, particularly in the British Parliament. This era of wool had been without violent competitive conflict with other sources of fabrics until cotton textiles of other regions of the world were brought to the attention of the English people. The Crusaders, impressed with the cotton fabrics they saw abroad, sent back samples of the beautiful cotton cloths of Palestine and other parts of the Middle East. Later, English adventurers sent home cotton from India.[13] Some of the cloth made by the Hindus was so gossamery that it was described as "webs of the woven wind." Garments made of the cloth could be drawn through a ring from a finger. So sheer were some of the cloths that a person wearing them appeared to be nude. Early in history the Hindus had developed a roller gin to separate seed from fibre.[14]

MORE CURSED THAN BLESSED

The English commenced to buy raw cotton and to spin and weave it by hand. As a result, a strong rivalry developed between the wool growers and weavers and the cotton textile operators. The more established wool industry sought comfort and relief through political pressure.[15]

In 1666, the Parliament decreed that the British dead would be buried exclusively in woolen shrouds.[16] In 1720, calico, made from cotton, was outlawed in England. People were forbidden to wear it.[17] But cotton cloth continued to grow in popularity. When efforts were made through political maneuvering to remove the English duty on the importation of raw cotton, the English flax spinners became concerned over the virginity of their maidens and the chastity of their wives. They said that cotton gave rise to erotic sensations.[18]

As the cotton industry gained over the wool producers, a cottage-village textile industry developed in England. Spinning and weaving plants were located in the individual homes in the villages. A cottage textile plant normally included one loom and sufficient raw cotton for a week's operation. Both old and young members of the households worked at the production of cotton cloth. The women and children did the gardening and spinning while the men did the heavier work. The family lived at home, grew a garden, and milked a cow.[19] But this happy existence of little people working in their own bailiwicks was threatened as steam power was applied to heavier textile equipment. With the innovation of steam power, a heavy textile industry developed in such large cities as Liverpool and Birmingham.[20]

As the young United States Republic grew stronger through the application of the gin to cotton production, England expanded its exports of cotton cloth from its new metropolitan textile centers. It was a blessing to England's economy but a bane to the villagers. The Hindus, who for thirty centuries had manufactured cotton into cloth by hand, discovered that they could not compete with the steam-fueled textile machinery of England.

The growth of English textile plants expanded the demand for more raw cotton from America. To meet this ever-increasing demand southern planters sought new ground to cultivate. The Indians had moved out of the Deep South, mostly to the Indian Territory, and the historic gong, so to speak, was sounded for the tempestous rush for unclaimed acres farther south. Every newcomer became a frontiersman, and frontier life involved violence. The Bowie knife was a symbol of authority in a perfidious period of American history.

The exodus of people from Maryland, Virginia, the Carolinas, and other parts of the nation to Georgia, Alabama, Mississippi, Louisiana, and adjacent areas created an era of confrontations and embroilments. Empassioned men were land hungry. They were seeking new land to replace the older land they had left behind, land made poor because of a type of farming which robbed the soil of its enrichment.[21] Planters gave little heed to the need of replacing the precious plant foods—nitrates, potash, and potassium—which were squandered in the plantation one-crop system of farming.

The extent of the exodus from the old South to the new South is reflected in this census report. In 1810 the combined population of Alabama and Mississippi was 40,000. In 1860 it was 1,660,000.[22] In the settling-down process wealth became concentrated in the hands of comparatively few. Only one third of the Deep South citizens were slave owners.[23]

The imposing homes in gracious settings were comparable to the "Castles on the Rhine" built during the days of feudalism in western Europe a thousand years before.[24] In these homes lived the South's aristocracy. Many were gentle people who lived in these mansions with the slave quarters in the rear. Among them were some people with an appreciation of learning and beautiful things—Italian marble, French art, Swedish chinaware, Oriental rugs, and Wycombe furniture. Many visited Europe in the winter, but all were under the influence of the Cotton Janus, the mold which was to form the character of the Deep South people of the twentieth century.

As the cotton acreage expanded, the price of slaves became inflated. A healthy, robust field hand was valued at $1,500. Infants were sold by the pound—$7 to $10 per pound, while boys and girls often were sold by height or weight.[25] Angry demands were heard for the re-opening of the slave markets of Africa where a good slave could be purchased for $50.[26]

The two thirds of the white people of the South who were not slaveowners competed with slaves for a livelihood. Slave labor set the basis upon which free white artisans were paid. The white carpenter competed with the black slave carpenter. In the market place he competed with the slaves hired out by their masters. The white brickmason competed with the black brickmason. The slave pattern was the enigma of free white people.

Logic, it would seem, should have impelled the non-slaveholders to realize the severe handicap which slavery forced upon them. But the plantation slaveowners were the leaders with the prestige and power. They controlled the thinking of the non-slaveholders. Those who owned no slaves offered little or no resistance to this pattern of thought control.

The non-slaveholders of the South were brain-washed by circumstances. They failed to comprehend that they were competing with the black slaves who were chattel. The white non-slaveholders were in a sense feudal slaves. The psychology which had prevailed along the Rhine and the Rhone rivers centuries before became the psychology which now prevailed along the Mississippi River, the Yazoo, the Suwannee, and the Atchafalaya rivers.

The white non-slaveholder worked his own fields. His lot in life—except for a limited number of unusually talented and ambitious persons—was economically unpromising. But the psychology which prevailed along the Rhine River in western Europe's years of feudalism prevailed in the Southland during its most critical slave days. And in the final hour of chaos and catastrophe, both slaveowners and non-slaveowners laid down their lives for a cause that could never win.

Another Cotton Janus curse was seen in the way of life of the South. It was a siren voice that lulled southern leaders into a stupor—an "easy agrarian way," an "intoxication with cotton," the leisurely, Bourbon-sipping life which somehow prevented the leaders from facing reality.[27] Leaders in the North and in the East, not affected with this leisurely approach to life and industry, capitalized upon the Cotton South.

Southern leaders not only complained of what they regarded as tribute exacted from their region by northern suppliers but also estimated what it had cost. The exaction for the period between 1800-1860 was placed at three billion dollars.[28]

The Cotton Janus had blessed the young American nation. No one would deny the timeliness of the blessing. Then came the evil years—the reversal of the South's trend toward emancipation. With increasingly worn-out soil, production dropped. Margins were narrowed. Southerners blamed their frustrations on the market, the supplier, colonial tribute, and the rigors of frontier life. But to be objective the question must be asked: were southern planters simply outsmarted or were these reversals the turning of the faces of Janus?

Romance as well as tragedy were associated with this Cotton Janus. Henry Grady, eloquent editor of the Atlanta *Constitution,* saw the cotton romance, the hibiscus in the cotton plant. "What a royal plant it is," he wrote.

> The world waits in attendance on its growth, the shower that falls whispering on its leaves is heard around the world, the sun that shines on it and the dew that

descends from the stars are noted, and the trespass of a little worm upon its green leaf is more to England than the advance of a hostile army on her Asian outpost. It is gold from the instant it puts forth its tiny shoot. Its fibre is currency in every bank, and when it fleeces to the sun, it floats a sunny banner that glorifies the fields of the humblest farmer that many is marshalled under a flag that will compel the allegiance of the world and bring a subsidy from every nation.

It could have been that the ready and assured cash market consistently waiting for the cotton to be picked may have appealed to Grady's poetic talents. It could have been that he was just another southerner unaccustomed to the face of reality. Or could it have been that he saw the lovelier of the two faces of Janus?

The greatest curse which this Cotton Janus saddled upon the people of the region was a philosophy intolerant of anything short of conformity; a philosophy of provincialism; a philosophy hostile to change because cotton in the beginning was accepted as for now and evermore; a philosophy of prejudices because it failed to distinguish between right and wrong.

A few far-sighted men of the Deep South recognized the growing curse of cotton. Sargent S. Prentiss, one of the Deep South's most eloquent statesmen, speaking in 1836 before the Mississippi legislature said, "We are legislating a loan for the present generation. Because we bask in a luxuriant soil and get good prices for our agriculture, we have no security that this will last. There are few things that can be produced on so great a portion of the earth's surface as cotton. Texas might, some day, surpass even Mississippi. South America will follow. If that day comes we should lament." [29]

For nearly one hundred years both whites and blacks in the Deep South did lament. But with time cotton left the hills. Much of it went to the broad valleys of the West. Diversification finally caught on, and with diversification came industry and a change of pace.

But the "cotton" thinking—the demand for conformity, the hostility to change, the acceptance of deep-seated racial prejudices, and the rationalism of "traditions"—were too deeply entrenched to be quickly eradicated.

NOTES TO CHAPTER 1

[1] David L. Cohn, *The Life and Times of King Cotton* (New York: Oxford University Press, 1956), 18.
[2] Wesley Frank Craven, *The Southern Colonies in the Seventeenth Century, 1607-1689* (Baton Rouge: Louisiana State University Press, 1949), 21.
[3] William B. Hesseltine, *The South in American History* (New York: Prentice-Hall, 1943), 156.
[4] Cohn, *Life and Times of King Cotton*, 21.
[5] Clement Eaton, *The Growth of Southern Civilization, 1790-1860* (New York: Harper and Brothers, 1961), 29.
[6] U.S. Department of Agriculture, *The Story of Cotton* (Consumer and Marketing Service, 1970).
[7] Eaton, *Growth of Southern Civilization*, 200.
[8] Cohn, *Life and Times of King Cotton*, 88.
[9] *Ibid.*, 17.   [10] *Ibid.*, 116.
[11] Dunbar Rowland, *History of Mississippi, The Heart of the South* (Chicago-Jackson: S. J. Clarke Publishing Co., 1925), 642.
[12] Hesseltine, *South in American History*, 157.
[13] Cohn, *Life and Times of King Cotton*, 18.   [14] *Ibid.*, 19.
[15] *Ibid.*, 18.   [16] Eaton, *Growth of Southern Civilization*, 162.
[17] U. S. Census Reports, 1810-1860.
[18] Clement Eaton, *The Mind of the Old South* (Baton Rouge: Louisiana State University Press, 1964), 90.

[19] Cohn, *Life and Times of King Cotton*, 60. [20] *Ibid.*, 91.
[21] C. Vann Woodward, *Origins of the New South, 1877–1913* (Baton Rouge: Louisiana State University Press, 1961), 110.
[22] Cohn, *Life and Times of King Cotton*, 90. [23] *Ibid.*, 87.
[24] *Compton's Encyclopedia*, V, 61. [25] *Ibid.*, 60. [26] *Ibid.*, 91.
[27] W. J. Cash, *The Mind of the South* (New York: Random House, 1960), 159.
[28] Cohn, *Life and Times of King Cotton*, 60.
[29] Clayton Rand, *Men of Spine in Mississippi* (Gulfport, Miss.: Dixie Press, 1940), 138.

2 Three Unforgettable Characters

THE TERM "unforgettable characters" has been popularized in print during the past couple of decades or so. Three characters will always be unforgettable to me. All three are dead. All three were humble people. All were black. And all three were victims of the cotton philosophy which prevailed with little inhibition in their days. Perhaps I should say that I am indebted to these humble people. In retrospect I learned some unforgettable lessons from them. I emphasize the words *in retrospect* because only in review, bulwarked by some personal soul-searching, have these lessons become apparent.

It was about the year 1912 when I first heard Howard Divinity speak to a small street gathering in my hometown, McComb, Mississippi. He was then an elderly man. I was a kid in what was then described as "short breeches."

Divinity's name had connotations which suggested that he was an ordained minister. A man named "Divinity" somehow just had to be a minister of the gospel. The black people referred to him as "the Reverend Howard Divinity," but at times doubt was expressed as to his spiritual qualifications to fill the pulpit.

Divinity's skin was ebony black. His whiskers and beard were snow white and he wore them in the style used by General Robert E. Lee in his lifetime. He was about the size and build of the famous general. He customarily wore a gray Confederate uniform. He usually was seen riding a gray mule and often he carried a rooster under his arm. His chest was covered with Confederate war medals.

Occasionally he went to the business area and immediately captured the attention of the people. When he spoke it was either from his saddle or standing beside his gray mule with bridle in hand. Usually he lambasted the "Damn Yankees," much to the entertainment of his southern listeners. It was generally understood that when he spoke he had a couple of shots of Bourbon whiskey under his belt. Merchants liked him and knew he liked whiskey. Why the rooster under his arm? Divinity claimed that during the war he had been the personal forager of "Marse" General Robert E. Lee. "The General liked chicken," said Divinity, "especially yellow-legged chickens. I carried a chicken about with me to be ready jest in case the General got hungry." Divinity possessed an impressive sense of forensic eloquence, particularly when he told of fighting side by side with the white "marsters" against the Yankees during the war. When asked if he had known General Stonewall Jackson, Divinity's eyes lighted up. He said, "I was with him at Bull Run. The Yankees were pressing us from all directions. The General stood straight up like a stone wall and looked them Yankees straight in the eyes. They didn't scare him none. That's why they called him Marse Stonewall Jackson. I know 'cause I was standing right there beside him."

On one occasion Divinity was hauled into court for

selling moonshine whiskey. The justice of the peace asked him, "Divinity, is it a fact that you sold that corn whiskey?" And Divinity replied, "Yes sir, Judge. It's true I sold that whiskey and most of the whiskey I sold to you." The judge sentenced him to three months in the town jail and that afternoon suspended the sentence.

One day Divinity became involved in a controversy with another member of his race. The other black man claimed he had saved the life of his "marster" during the war when he had stepped in front of his white "marster" just in time to intercept a bullet and hence save his life. Divinity resented anyone competing with him for the spotlight. Standing against his gray mule, he told his crowd with an obvious show of emotion, "That's a damn lie. No southern white man would let a nigger stand in front of him." This pleased his crowd as Divinity knew it would.

No one ever knew where Divinity got his war medals. Although the question was asked, no one pressed him for an answer. His medals, his Confederate uniform, his gray mule, the rooster under his arm, and his raw eloquence made something of a hero of the Reverend Howard Divinity.

In 1922 the members of the local post of the American Legion paid his expenses and took him to the national convention in New Orleans where his showmanship won him new friends. The following year, another group of legionnaires paid his expenses to the national convention held in San Francisco. His fame grew. The late lieutenant-governor, Dennis Murphree of Mississippi, took Divinity aboard the "Know Mississippi Better" train which toured the nation and carried with it an exhibit of Mississippi-made products.

Even after he became an octogenarian, Divinity, with his characteristic braggadocio and good humor would say, "I can go into a chicken house on the darkest night and pick out the fattest hen on the roost." Then he would add parenthetically that he still knew good whiskey when he tasted it.

Many old Confederate veterans were alive during my boyhood. Throughout the Deep South, county Confederate veterans' reunions were held annually. Divinity was invited to a number of them where he lambasted the "Damn Yankees," fawned on the Confederacy, and invariably passed his Confederate cap through the crowd.

A stenographer who worked in a realtor's office told me that for an extended period of time Divinity's wife lived two counties away. He remained in a servant's cabin and looked after a physician's horse and garden. The lady said that during this period of separation she helped him by typing letters to his wife. "Invariably," she said, "he would start his letters, 'My dear wife Susan' and would end them 'Your devoted husband, Howard.'" These letters somehow revealed an inner sense of dignity not evinced in his general masquerade.

What was the lesson I belatedly learned from Howard Divinity?

The truth I did not know then, and which others did not suspect, was that Divinity's act was an act of survival. He doubtlessly recognized the practicability of playing a role in which he sacrificed all aspects of human dignity.

THREE UNFORGETTABLE CHARACTERS

People laughed, but his life was one of pathos. He played the part of a buffoon because it was his way of conforming to the system, a system deeply etched in the mores, the customs, and the prejudices of the people. Divinity possessed intelligence. If his whiskers had been black and his skin white, rather than the reverse, conceivably he could have succeeded in politics. After all, he knew what the people wanted to hear and said it. And this technique has been the foundation of many successful Deep South political careers.

In retrospect, the most profound lesson I learned from Howard Divinity was that I personally was a part of this system of human degradation.

The second black person in this trio of unforgettable characters was Bob Harvey. He was a large, round-faced man who weighed more than 250 pounds. I recall his black, shiny face, always smiling and usually wet with sweat. He drove a team of horses hitched to a wagon owned by Frank McIntosh, the town's only drayman.

Bob was gentle-hearted. He liked youngsters. One day long ago he said, "Mr. Mac, my bossman, is the only man in the world who slops his pigs in a gold pigpen." He was almost correct. A one-ring circus came to town and incurred some debts it could not pay. One of the creditors was the town drayman. Armed with a judgment, Mr. McIntosh went to the circus tent to see what he could get in settlement of his account. Among the bizarre equipment was a highly ornamented and gilded lion's cage on wheels. He hitched a team of mules to the ornate cage and hauled it to his home place. He put his hogs in the gilded cage, and while his swine consisted of ordinary, native stock it could truthfully be said that no pedigreed Poland China hog anywhere could have had a more flamboyant and majestic pig castle in which to grunt the days away.

Bob Harvey was a friend to the youngsters of town. He would drive his wagon along a street near a sandlot where kids were playing baseball and all of them would yell, "Hi, Bob." And Bob would yell back from amidst the dust he had stirred in the road, "Hey dere, Hey dere." Each youngster in his enthusiasm wanted to be recognized personally; so Bob would yell back, "I hear you. I hear you, too." In time Bob acquired the nickname "I hear you, too, Bob Harvey."

In that day many, many families of McComb ordered staple groceries from New Orleans, 105 miles to the south, and about once a month had them shipped on the Illinois Central Railroad. Bob was in a position to know when these grocery orders arrived, since it was his job to deliver them.

R. E. Edwards, a machinist in the railroad shops, always ordered a fifth of Bourbon whiskey for himself and a bottle of port wine for his wife. Bob not only delivered groceries to the Edwards family but stopped there regularly to pick up scraps for his pigs. When the Edwards groceries arrived, Bob delivered them pronto. A member of the Edwards household recalling Bob Harvey at grocery delivery time, told me that Bob had what was almost a ritual when Mr. Edwards offered him a drink. "We always gave him a small drink," she said, "but before imbibing he would drop to his knees and make the sign of the cross. After the

THREE UNFORGETTABLE CHARACTERS

whiskey was well blessed, he drank it with gusto and drama."

In later years I saw Bob high upon a wagon loaded with second-hand lumber. The mule was having a difficult time pulling the load. Some of the lumber extended beyond the end of the wagon body and dragged on the ground. Observing his 250 pounds of avoirdupois on top of the load, I admonished him. "Bob," I said, "you should not be riding on this load. That lumber is too heavy for your mule to pull even without you riding on top of it."

With characteristic guffaws, Bob replied in a loud, laughing voice, "That's a goodern on you, Boss. This old mule don't know I'm up here. He's blind."

The lesson I learned in retrospect from Bob Harvey was that his boisterousness, his guffaws, and his exaggerated joviality were not simply factors of his personality. It was his way of living by his wits. Many regarded him as a clown. Actually his manners expressed his cunning. Doubtless he recognized the odds against him because he was black, and he realized that his best approach to life was to rely on his cunning and to live by his wits. And he did.

The third of this trio of black persons was "Sis" Bickham. Her husband Frank came from East Fork, a rural community in Amite County. Her mother Maria acted as the babysitter while Sis served as the wash and scrubwoman of the neighborhood. Her hands were in suds and water more often than they were out. She worked for a different family each day of the week. The three important but inanimate things in Sis's life were the big black washpots in every backyard in her day, the scrubbing board over which she bent many hours of every week, and the flatiron she used to press clothes after she washed them. She used old-fashioned charcoal type furnaces to heat her flatirons on what was called "ironing day."

Often Maria would accompany Sis to look after the grandchildren while Sis worked. If one of the children became too mischievous Maria would call out, "Youngern, bring me your back." Then she usually lightly paddled the offending youngster.

Frank, Sis's husband, was very proud of a blue coat which some white friend had given him. One day he was summoned to appear in the justice of the peace's court and charged with robbing a hen house. The prosecuting attorney knew about Frank's blue coat and the pride associated with it. Knowing also that Frank was somewhat simple-minded, he asked Frank as he sat in the witness chair, "Frank, did you wear your pretty blue coat the night you robbed the hen house?" Frank replied, "No sir, I was in my shirt sleeves the night I robbed the hen house."

A family by the name of Tucker had a black man on their place who preached on Sundays. He was called "Toodle Mouth" by the black people because when he preached he had a peculiar way of rolling his lips inside out. Sis Bickham discovered she could roll her lips in the way the preacher did and with this accomplishment she clowned before the white folk. "I've got toodle mouth lips," she would say. "I'm de precher. Hear me. Praise the Lord." Then she would roll her lips inside out as the people around her laughed.

Whenever Sis had a new baby she would name it after

some person from whom she reasonably could expect a gift. One of her children she named Oliver. Sis went to my mother and said, "I've named my baby after your little boy." Then quickly she came to the point. "What you gonna gimme for my baby?" My mother responded with a gift for the baby. Then Sis called on the wife of a railroadman named Oliver Williams. "I've named my new child, Oliver, after your husband. What you gonna gimme for my baby?"

The mayor at the time was Dr. Oliver B. Quin. Sis repeated the story to the mayor's wife and then asked, "What you gonna gimme for my baby?" The idea somehow infuriated Mrs. Quin. She reached for a broom and drove Sis off her premises. Usually, however, the gifts were forthcoming.

When Sis was in a backyard she usually had an apple box under a tree. There she kept the youngest of her family while she worked over the scrub-board and the big black washpot.

Sis was loud-mouthed and boisterous. When she talked you could hear her all over the neighborhood. Most of the stories she told were bawdy. But she labored hard, loved her children, and reared her brood with sweat, hard work, cunning, and a love knitted to sacrifice.

Years later, at a ripe old age, Sis Bickham died. Remembering her difficult years, I published a gentle tribute to her memory in my front page column of the McComb *Enterprise-Journal.*

The following day an alert, neatly dressed young man walked into my office. He was the principal of a high school. He said, "You perhaps do not know me. My mother was Sis Bickham whom you wrote about in your newspaper yesterday. I want to thank you for the kind things you said about her." His English was correct. His personality was clear-cut and not without dignity. He was one of the babies who in earlier years lay in the apple box and looked up into the green leaves of the trees above.

The lesson I had learned from Sis Bickham in retrospect is obvious. Her son was the evidence of the lesson. Despite a cruel, even degrading, background, Sis Bickham reared a worthy son. His personality and work in his profession proved that his mother had made the world better than she had found it. Yet she, like Howard Divinity and Bob Harvey, was a child of slavery.

To have been born and reared in the Deep South was to accept and embrace its prejudices, not deliberately, not consciously, not even knowingly, but subconsciously, just as the white-blossomed dogwoods, the redbud trees, and the longleaf yellow pines are accepted as part of the Deep South scenery and as the midnight chorus of the mockingbird and the morning calls of the towhee, the wren, and the brown thrasher are accepted as the sounds of the region. The alternative to conformity was to live under the suspicion of disloyalty.

This complexity of misunderstanding and misinterpretation perpetuated a costly and erroneous premise—the premise that the people of the Deep South understood the Negro. The truth is that Deep South people understood the black man least of all.

3 Lesson in Retrospect

IN THE EARLY thirties I read that Dr. E. Stanley Jones, noted Methodist missionary, was scheduled to speak at Millsaps College in Jackson, Mississippi. At that time he was already recognized for his understanding of racial problems and his deep concern for those unfortunate people stymied by the caste system, especially in India, home of the "untouchables."

I wrote to Dr. Jones at Cincinnati, Ohio, and told him I had a question I wanted to ask him and said I would appreciate it if he would permit me time to talk with him while he was in Jackson. He replied with the graciousness for which he was known and suggested that I meet him in his room at the Walthall Hotel following his lecture at the college.

On the scheduled evening I heard his message and later joined him in his hotel room. After a few moments of customary pleasantries he asked me, "What is that important question you want to ask me?"

I first explained that I regarded him as one of the best-informed men in America on matters of racial conflict. Then I said, "I know it may seem somewhat ridiculous to ask you a question about Negroes voting when so little interest today is being manifested in the subject." Then I asked this question: "When the time arrives that black people will demand the right to vote—and achieve this right—will they, in your judgment, vote as a bloc or will they vote as individuals?"

Without hesitation Dr. Jones replied, "That depends upon whether they are treated as Negroes or whether they are treated as citizens. If we treat them as black people they will vote as a bloc, but if we treat them as citizens the conservative blacks will vote with the conservative whites and the liberal blacks will vote with the liberal white persons." Then he added, "If the emphasis is upon citizenship there will be little change in the political structure as a result of extending the right of franchise to black people."

Then Dr. Jones said something which made a profound and lasting impression upon me, a thought which was to become a guiding light to me during the turbulent years ahead when black leadership would demand the constitutional right of franchise. Observed Dr. Jones, "In every recorded civilization leadership has been divided into two kinds, the conservatives on the one hand and the liberals on the other and all progress has been born out of the clashes between these two leaderships. Whenever in history the conservatives became too reactionary the masses went over to the liberals and whenever the liberals became too radical the masses moved back to the conservatives." Then he added, "You will find that the black people are no exception to this rule of history."

I left Dr. E. Stanley Jones's room that night feeling deeply indebted to him. To me it was an edifying experience.

LESSON IN RETROSPECT

A few weeks later I dropped by the Mississippi State Department of Education and talked with Dr. Percy Easom, the official in charge of Negro education in the state. I related to him the conversation I had with Dr. Jones.

At that time people throughout the South were still growing cotton in the hills. Cotton was the major crop and primary source of cash for the farmer as well as the businessman. It was the basis of the South's economy.

Dr. Easom, after hearing my report on Dr. Jones's comment as to how the black people would vote when that day in history arrived, asked me, "Do you know who is the most conservative person in Mississippi today?"

The question caught me somewhat by surprise. I confessed that I didn't know. He replied, "It is the Negro landowner." I asked him to explain.

He replied, "A Negro landowner doesn't want to change anything. He doesn't want to sign any papers. If a petition is circulated dealing with roads or other public matters he will think a long time and talk to his most trusted friends before signing it. He reacts just as most of the white people do when any change is suggested. He's a disciple of the status quo."

This conversation with the director of Negro education in the state of Mississippi reinforced my confidence in the statement made by Dr. Jones. If the black man, when given his constitutional right to vote, were treated as a citizen, it became conceivable that the white conservative and the black conservative would vote together as would the white and black liberals. Under these circumstances no massive political changes would likely come to pass after the first few years of the black man's adjustment to his newly acquired franchise.

The question rightly could be asked, why in the early thirties was I concerned with the proposition of black franchise? Little thought was directed toward such a goal at that time. Certainly I did not possess uncanny foresight. On the contrary, over the years I have manifested far too great a lack of it. But I have always enjoyed the thrilling reminders of the colonial Americans who founded our country—the story of the Boston Tea Party, the "Give me liberty or give me death" speech of Patrick Henry, the glorious moments of July 4, 1776, when our revolutionary forebears signed the Declaration of Independence.

The principle of "taxation without representation" stirred the fervor and the souls of the early Americans and was the powder keg which exploded in the faces of the representatives of King George and established freedom on this continent. There was every reason to believe that the stage of 1776 would be reset, that the same drama would be reenacted in the twentieth century. The same principle would be involved—"taxation without representation."

The blacks were taxed. No one could argue to the contrary. True, they were poorer than most whites and paid fewer taxes. But they were, nevertheless, taxpayers. As taxpayers in the Deep South they were not represented because they were not allowed to vote or hold office. Once again, America was confronted with the same principle which had led to Cornwallis' surrender to General

LESSON IN RETROSPECT

George Washington at Yorktown. The same emotion which had aroused Jefferson, Franklin, and Patrick Henry at Williamsburg would inevitably be aroused in the minds of disfranchised people nearly two centuries later.

Why was it that the people in the Deep South could not foresee the inevitability of the conflict ahead? Perhaps we were blinded by our own lack of comprehension, our own failure to recognize that principles remain constant despite race. Perhaps we were trying to keep the sentiments of a dead century or were warped in judgment by our determined resistance to change. We were wed to the status quo and were in no mood to accept a divorce.

Actually, my question to Dr. Jones was, "What can we expect when the inevitable conflict comes to a head?"

His answer was prophetic. Principles stand. Today blacks are voting. They have moved into the mainstream of politics in the Deep South. No one can deny this. More adjustments are yet to be made. But the fear of a bloc vote is lessening as more and more black and white conservatives vote together and more and more black and white liberals share the same political philosophy.

4 The Dipping Vat War

WHEN NOT AROUSED emotionally, Deep South folk are gentle, friendly, neighborly, and exceedingly accommodating people. When stirred by bitter controversy they can become angry, stubborn people with the militancy of a nest of hornets.

In earlier years in this region people agonized over a bug —the blood-sucking Texas cattle tick. When this parasite (*margaropus annulatus*) attacked, neither milk nor beef could be produced profitably, although the people desperately need both.[1*] A program launched to eradicate cattle ticks proved to be not only arduous and irritatingly time-consuming in its application but was fraught with frustrations which put the nerves of thousands of people on edge. The program was started during World War I and was not terminated until the year 1929.

The federal government cooperated with the states to eradicate this costly pest. Since part of the life cycle of the cattle tick is lived on cattle and horses, public vats were built and filled with arsenic solution. Law made it mandatory that all people dip their cattle, horses, and mules every two weeks. The conflict between the goal of developing the cattle industry in the Deep South on the one hand and the hard grind and grime of dipping on the

* Notes appear at end of chapter.

other created a dilemma. The dipping vat became a factor in the lives of the people. It was something of an oversize human barometer which measured the reaction of Deep South people to pressure, emotions, and change.

Recently, I decided to interview a number of persons who remembered those feverish years. Since women live longer than men I discussed the subject with more women than men. Nevertheless I interviewed many men who had played an active part in this program.

Rodney Foreman, for many years a resident of Amite County, Mississippi, said to me, "I can remember the night that people had become so exasperated with the dipping situation that it was decided to dynamite seventeen vats in the county on one night." A vat, incidentally, was a concrete trench deep enough to submerge a full grown steer. It was roofed and had two side walls with a gate at each end. Then he went into the details of the plan and how it was executed. "There were three or four men named to dynamite each dipping vat. It was agreed," explained Foreman, "that all of the vats should be dynamited at exactly the same time. The vat at Liberty, the county seat, failed to 'go off' but seventeen vats in all were blown to smithereens that fateful night."

Foreman said that one reason the dynamiters were so irritated was the charge that owners of large herds were not being forced to dip but that all small farmers were being made to come up to the "lick log." "Then too," he said, "often young stock were blistered by the dipping solution, especially on their undersides." [2]

Higdon Hutson, a retired farmer, told me that as a young

man he was a range rider with the eradication program. He considered the range in Smith County too dangerous to ride alone.[3] He said, "On one weekend between noon on Saturday and midnight on Sunday in our county twenty-seven vats were dynamited. The people in the county where I worked lit more fuses and exploded more dynamite than they did in Amite County."

Hutson added that the government provided a range rider for roughly every twelve dipping vats. "A dipping inspector kept a record of all cattle dipped. As each head of livestock came out of the vat it was daubed with paint," he said. He further explained, "We used red, green, and yellow paint. At each dipping we used a different color of paint on a different part of the animal's body. This enabled the rangers to travel over the area and determine which cattle had not been dipped. No one knew until the last minute which color of paint we would use or on what part of the body. Otherwise many, many people would have remained away from the dipping vats and painted their own cattle."[4]

Horses and mules were dipped. I learned that some horses were too large to go through the standard dipping vat. In such cases the dipping officials used buckets to wash the animals in the solution, making certain that they were well drenched between their legs.

I was told that a citizen of Summit, Mississippi, had a dairy cow he refused to dip or have dipped. A ranger called at the home, loaded the cow on a truck, and transported her to the county seat where she was impounded. Later the man was fined and charged for the transportation of his cow to the vat. This happened each time for three dipping periods. During the fourth period he personally delivered his pedigreed cow to the dipping vat.

A lady, recalling the dipping debacle, reported that the dipping inspectors insisted that her mother's horse be dipped. She refused and said, "The horse is out there. If you want to dip him you can do it. I won't." The inspector took the horse to the dipping vat. The animal became frightened, attempted to leap across the length of the vat, and broke his neck. Later the government paid the lady a hundred dollars for the loss of her horse.[5]

One lady told me that her father was a tick eradication inspector. "My grandfather," she said, "called him the 'radication inspector.'" The extent of work involved in dipping cattle can be appraised from her statement. She said, "My father would get up at three in the morning and drive a mule to a buggy. Dipping started at dawn. Meanwhile farmers were out before dawn to drive their cattle from the open range to the vats. After the farmers arrived at the dipping vats they had to await their respective turns at dipping and then spend added time in the dripping pens where the stock were daubed with colored paint with the use of a long-handled stiff brush."[6]

There were some Texas longhorn cattle in the region. These wide horns made it difficult to get them through the vats. After these cattle were roped, the task required some strong, agile men to hold the heads of the longhorns in an oblique position while other strong men pushed and pulled them through the vats. Obviously, such arduous tasks did not contribute to the popularity of dipping.

One lady told me, "I lived through the dipping vat war. My family constantly feared for the life of my father."

Another lady said to me, "I can remember when the vats were built. My father built his own. He had 640 acres of land and a large number of cattle. But they blew up his vat, too."

Another lady commented, "I heard the vats exploding, one right after another. I could see the flares of some that were near where I lived."

Still another reminisced, "My father was a law enforcement officer. There were threats made against him. They told him if he did not tell them where a certain dipping vat inspector was hiding that they would kill him." She said her father replied, "Well, you will just have to go ahead and kill me." "But he lived," she said somewhat proudly.

A veteran of World War I said to me, "One of the troubles was that many farmers refused to believe that it was tick fever that was killing their cattle." After returning from France he inspected his own cattle and found them so covered with ticks they looked as if they were wearing a coat of armor. Many people said that ticks often were on cattle in such masses that it was difficult to determine the color of an animal.[7]

One lady, learning I was interviewing people who had been involved in the dipping war, wrote to me. She said, "My father did not blow up our vat. He took a top maul and 'busted' it up. It belonged to my grandfather at that time."[8]

The immensity of the task of dipping cattle is reflected

in the statistics of just one county—Amite County, where seventeen vats were dynamited in one night. This county had thirty dipping inspectors and range riders who dipped 24,678 head of cattle and 6,463 head of horses and mules every two weeks in 173 dipping vats in a program which was spread over several years.[9]

The value of cattle during the time of tick infestation can be calculated from an advertisement which was published in the *Southern Herald* of Liberty, Mississippi, by the coroner, A. G. Stratton, on August 8, 1928. He had picked up a stray Hereford cow weighing 700 pounds which had been appraised "by a committee of three men" at approximately $20.00. Obviously it was valued at 2.86 cents per pound.[10] Good beef could not be produced when cattle were infested with ticks.

A program which aroused such intense feeling and which proved so frustrating was by no means bloodless. There were casualties listed across the Deep South.

In the year 1929, after years of dipping cattle, the tick eradication program slowed to an end. Then a new aspect of the problem presented itself. Although the state of Mississippi became "tick free," the state of Louisiana did not.

To keep Louisiana's ticky cattle out of Mississippi was simple in that area where the Mississippi River separates the two states. But the problem was not so simple in southwest Mississippi where the ticky cattle from Louisiana could walk across the state line and reinfest cattle in the state of Mississippi and undo the work of the long, hard years required to eradicate these pests. At this juncture a completely new story came to the surface.

Along the border of southwest Mississippi and southeast Louisiana are the counties of Pearl River, Marion, Walthall, Pike, Amite, and Wilkinson. The Pike County Board of Supervisors decided to employ guards around the clock to patrol the border on horseback. Each guard was to be assigned one mile as a beat. His task would be to keep Louisiana cattle out of the county along his beat, riding regularly from one end of his beat to the other. Each guard was scheduled to ride eight hours per day. Hence three shifts per mile per day was to be required for thirty miles, necessitating a total of ninety guards.[11]

This arrangement impressed me as being both impractical and extravagant. If a guard were on the east end of his mile-long beat, a ticky Louisiana steer could easily walk across the state line at the west end and fade into the woodlands without detection before the guard could return.

As a newspaper editor, I opposed the board's employing mounted guardsmen. I held that it was an impractical approach to the proposition and said that the political patronage involved had influenced the board's decision. Instead the editorial suggestion was made that a double-line fence be built between the two states. The estimated cost for the fence required along the county line was $6,800, less than the cost of one month's salaries for the ninety guards proposed.

The president of the county board, "Uncle John" Gatlin, a deeply religious man and a politically influential individual, resented the things I had said and, backed by his board, published a letter in a county seat newspaper in which he referred to me as a "Young Whippersnapper." Webster defines a whippersnapper as "an insignificant, presumptuous person." Since *Time* magazine had published the controversy between the young editor and the board—and glamorized the idea of an editor trying to fence one state away from another—I have an idea that the term "whippersnapper" was justifiably used.

The controversy came to a head at a mass meeting in the town hall in McComb where the idea of building the fence was endorsed. The specifications adopted were as follows: "Double wire fence of 4 strands each, 4 pt. heavy cattle wire, 15 feet apart, along the state line between Louisiana and Mississippi for approximately 30 miles. Posts 10 feet apart, heart pine, white oak, locust, cherry and 6½ feet long, 2 feet in the ground and wire securely nailed to said posts and staples." [12]

The supervisors built a fence along the state line as did the boards of the nearby counties. Roughly 150 miles of double fence were built between the two states.[13] In time the state of Louisiana became "tick-free."

This dipping vat war was not just a war against the cattle tick. It was a war favoring the status quo. Despite the general philosophy against change the status quo lost. In Mississippi it was a thirteen-year war. The legislature enacted the first compulsory dipping law in 1916.[14] The state became tick free in 1929. Obviously the people resented being forced to do anything—even if it helped them.

The dates of the battles with the cattle tick did not coincide exactly in all of the states involved. In Alabama, for instance, the program was started in 1914. Considerable difficulties were encountered, particularly in the field of litigation. Records indicate that seventeen cases were carried to the supreme court.[15]

The fences between Louisiana and Mississippi, no longer needed, eventually rotted. After the ticks were eradicated cattle thrived. The old scrub bulls that had wandered over the open range were replaced by quality sires. Pastures were fenced. The open range became a thing of history. The soil was seeded with improved grasses.

Today where the "tick fences" were built are to be found some of the world's finest dairy herds, some of the world's most sophisticated dairy equipment, and thousands of pedigreed beef and dairy cattle—all the result of change.

NOTES TO CHAPTER 4

[1] *Mississippi Code Annotated Recompiled* (Atlanta: Harrison Co., 1956), IV, 4852.
[2] Conversation with author, McComb, Mississippi, November 26, 1971.
[3] Conversation with author, Johnston Station, Mississippi, December 1, 1971.   [4] *Ibid.*
[5] Mrs. Bobbye Barnett in conversation with author, McComb, Mississippi, February 10, 1972.
[6] Mrs. Selma Moak in conversation with author, Enterprise Community, Summit, Mississippi, December 1, 1971.
[7] Ernest Jackson in conversation with author, McComb, Mississippi, November 25, 1971.
[8] Mrs. Glover May, Summit, Mississippi, to author, November 10, 1971.
[9] Biennial Report of Mississippi Livestock Sanitary Board (Jackson, 1928–29), 4.
[10] Liberty (Miss.) *Southern Herald*, August 31, 1928.
[11] McComb (Miss.) *City Enterprise*, April 12, 1929.
[12] Liberty (Miss.) *Southern Herald*, September 27, 1929.
[13] Information from Office of State Veterinarian, Jackson, Mississippi, May 23, 1972.

[14] John K. Bettersworth, *Mississippi—A History* (Austin, Tex.: Steck Co., 1959), 400.
[15] Information from J. G. Miligan, Alabama State Veterinarian, in letter to author, May 23, 1972.

5 High Cost of Demagoguery

JUST BEFORE THE turn of the nineteenth century and during the early decades of the twentieth, the Southland in general and the cotton country of the Deep South in particular were tragically troubled with political demagogues.

The term *demagogue*, according to Webster's dictionary, means a "leader who makes use of popular prejudices and false claims and promises in order to gain power."

Using the tactics of the itinerant patent medicine salesman who staged shows to help peddle his wares, these demagogues bewitched, beguiled, cajoled, deceived, tricked, and misled the gullible people to the point that the demagogues contributed to a philosophy of backwardness which in time prevailed throughout the Deep South. This stultifying philosophy destroyed the area's best interests, kept the people in ignorance, and perpetuated illiteracy.

These demagogues preached from the Bible, praised the founding fathers, extolled the virtues of General Robert E. Lee and Confederate President Jefferson Davis, commended all veterans of the Confederacy, protested the nigger-loving damn Yankees, purveyed coarse jokes, anecdotes, and histrionics, and captured both the votes and the hearts of the people.[1]* They used the Negro and Wall Street as their whipping boys.

* Notes appear at end of chapter.

HIGH COST OF DEMAGOGUERY

The white people, tied to the poverty-perpetuating, one-crop cotton system, reacted as if they believed the demagogues could stop the sun. But the only thing they stopped was the progress of the Southland.

James K. Vardaman of the state of Mississippi was high on the list of these apostles of showmanship, political drama, and the preachments of hate. Vardaman, ignoring Abraham Lincoln's proclamation of emancipation and the United States Constitution, kept alive the spirit of slavery, a system which had debased the South and forced whites to compete with slave labor. He cried out from the political stump, "The way to control the nigger is to whip him when he does not obey without it and another is to pay him no more than is actually necessary to buy food and clothes." [2]

Vardaman, often spoken of as the "Negro-cussin' Vardaman," referred to himself as the "Great White Chief." He let his hair grow long. His charcoal black locks draped gracefully across his shoulders. He dressed himself completely in white—white suit, white shirt, white tie, white hat, and white shoes, symbolical of white supremacy—and when attending political rallies rode into town on a multi-yoke oxwagon drawn by pure white oxen.[3]

Vardaman set himself up as the champion of the farmer against predatory corporate interests. Moneyed interests, he believed, ruled the world for selfish ends. Bankers and railroads he saw as locusts devouring the farmer by usurious and exorbitant rates. The wealthy, he said, are "conscienceless and insatiable. They never get enough and know not the corrective pangs of remorse." [4]

The "Great White Chief" deplored the state's school system. He concluded there were too many people to educate. He disliked the fact that there were more schools and better paid teachers in the Delta than in the hills. He declared Negro children were getting educated while many white children were not. Negroes, he claimed, were paying less than 5 percent of the school fund. The children of the races, he thought, should be educated not according to school attendance but according to the taxes paid by whites and blacks. He ran for governor and was elected on this platform. At the turn of the century, he said, no white man was willing for the Negro to reach a higher social, economic, or political level than he enjoyed. The state ostensibly was paying a half million dollars a year for Negro education to equip them for "the duties of citizenship." But, said Vardaman, after several million dollars have been spent, and the Negro has been taught to read and write, he would then want to vote. He would not, however, be permitted to do so. "His vote will either be cast aside or Sambo will vote as directed by the white folks." There's no use multiplying words about it, Vardaman concluded. Money spent to educate the Negro is a "positive unkindness to him." [5] It simply renders him unfit to work as "the white man has prescribed, and which he will be forced to perform."

"The Negro," he said, was "a curse to the country" and had cost it more than "all the wars it has waged added to the ruin wrought by flood and fire." "Moreover," he said, "the black man was an industrial stumbling block, a political ulcer, a social scab and a lazy, lying, lustful animal which no amount of training can transform into a tolerable citizen. His nature," declared the demagogue, "was unlike the white man's and resembles the hog's."

This essence of man's inhumanity to man helped to lay the groundwork for the racial problems of the last half of the twentieth century. People were thus tutored in the ways of inhumanity because the demagogue determined the rule of conduct in broad sections of the country.

Vardaman was crude, insulting, and degrading in his references to the black people. He gave quasi defense of lynching during his campaign and later called it the "natural product of unnatural conditions." But during his first year as governor, he called out the state militia at a cost of $250,000, ordered special railroad trains, took personal command, and rushed to Washington County to protect two Negroes threatened with mob action.[6] The Natchez *Democrat* observed, "Almost every white man indulged in the hope that the mob would do its work." [7] The national press, including the New York *Times*, the Brooklyn *Eagle*, and the Chicago *Tribune*, commended Vardaman for his action.[8]

But Vardaman was only one of many demagogues. Texas had her "Pa" and "Ma" Ferguson. Fergusonism spread over the Lone Star State as Vardamanism had swept over Mississippi. On July 21, 1917, the Travis County grand jury indicted Governor Jim Ferguson on nine charges, most of them pertaining to misapplication of funds.[9] He countered by calling his adversaries "little tin Jesuses" and "two-bit thieves." Meanwhile, the Texas senate sustained ten of twenty-one articles of impeachment passed by the house; and Jim Ferguson, son of a poor Methodist minister, could no longer hold any Texas office of "honor, trust or profit." [10]

But Jim Ferguson was a resourceful demagogue. He asked the people of Texas to vindicate him. He took to the stump and campaigned the state for the election of Miriam Wallace Ferguson, his wife, and promised that Texas could have two governors for the price of one. Soon the "Ma" and "Pa" team was back in the political saddle again. Although she became the governor, "Pa" Ferguson was governor by proxy.

Louisiana had the "Kingfish," Huey P. Long, who served as a United States senator while he was still the governor of the state of Louisiana. He preached sharing of the wealth and promised to make every man a king. Brilliant, dynamic, eloquent, and resourceful, he could compete with any rabble-rouser in America. He studied carefully the tactics of his neighbor, Theodore G. Bilbo of Mississippi. The "Kingfish" was proud of the multi-storied Louisiana capitol which he built on the banks of the Mississippi River. He said, "Only one building compares with its architecture. That's the St. Peter's Cathedral in Rome." [11]

Allan Michie and Frank Rhylick, who made a study of Dixie demagogues, wrote of Huey Long: "When the wind is from the south there are Cajuns in Louisiana who stand outside their huts and listen expectantly. Sometimes they only hear the rustling of the loblolly pines or the ripple of the water among the reeds on the shore of the bayou. But if the wind is strong and howls through the treetops like a restless spirit, they say they hear Huey

Long. He's telling them that the monument on his grave in Baton Rouge is not heavy enough to keep him from coming back to ease their burdens." [12] It was said of Huey Long that on the stump his peculiar genius combined "the story-telling of Tom Heflin, the evangelical fervor of Bilbo, and the musical appeal of W. Lee O'Daniel, with the billingsgate of a dock walloper and the raucous humor of a bawdy-house keeper" which provided rare entertainment in the uneventful lives of the Louisiana Cajun people. There are students of politics in America today who believe that had Huey Long not been felled by an assassin's bullet his special brand of demagoguery would have carried him to the White House. In 1935 Long planned to run as an independent candidate for president. He no doubt had an eye focused on the White House. Shortly before he was assassinated he said, "We are building up an organization in the country like we have in Louisiana. I already have Mississippi and Arkansas. I can take Alabama when I am ready. There positively will be a 'Share-our-Wealth' ticket." [13]

"Pitchfork Ben" Tillman of South Carolina got his nickname when he made the effort to go to Washington. "Send me to Washington," he yelled to the frantic crowds, "and I'll stick my pitchfork in his [the president's] ribs." [14] He presented to the nation a series of addresses in the senate and on the Chataqua platform, the views of southern extremists regarding the race question. He justified the lynching of Negroes in cases of rape and advocated the use of force in disenfranchising them.

"Pitchfork Ben" brought his "nigger baiting" clear

along the brutal course. And after him virtually the whole host of demagogues, in their turn, would owe their success to their capacity to arouse the racial prejudices of the people.

Eugene Talmadge carried the title, "the Wild Man of Sugar Creek, Georgia." His political trademarks were his unruly forelocks of ebony black hair, his gaudy red galluses, his Harold Lloyd spectacles, and his cracker accent.[15] He emphasized his oratory by snapping his suspenders as he exploited the fears of the farmers and their deeply ingrained prejudices and suspicions. The "Wild Man from Sugar Creek," militant advocate of white supremacy, was heralded as the most dynamic force in Georgia since the Populist demagogue, Thomas E. Watson.

Alabama had her era of the flamboyant "Cotton Tom" Heflin, who in his black coat, white vest, flowing necktie, and pince-nez spun yarns and hurled invectives as the rabble excitedly shouted approval.

Joe Cannon, who held forth for years as the Speaker of the House in Congress and as an after-dinner humorist, compared "Cotton Tom" Heflin to an Alabama sunset. He observed, "An Alabama sunset is a string of big, red, fat fire crackers all going off at the same time"—an apt description of most of the demagogues who have influenced the politics, and hence the well-being or the lack of it, in the Deep South during the past decades.[16]

Demagogues usually selected campaign titles with as much careful consideration as great corporations give to selecting names for new commercial products they launch upon the market—"Pitchfork Ben" Tillman; "Kingfish"

HIGH COST OF DEMAGOGUERY

Huey Long; the "Great White Chief" Jim Vardaman; "the Man" Bilbo, also called "the Stormy Petrel;" "Ma" and "Pa" Ferguson; "the Wild Man of Sugar Creek," Gene Talmadge; "Pass-the-Biscuits, Pappy" O'Daniel of Texas; "Tom Tom" Heflin; and "Alfalfa Bill" Murray all pursued this course. The name "Alfalfa Bill" fit well with his shaggy hair, his wild mustache, and the wild, new pioneer Oklahoma country.

The demagogues of the early part of the century all possessed a certain distinctiveness, but by no means were they all alike. Yet they all exhibited a pattern of certain characteristics. They inflamed the emotions of the people. They were students of the frustrations of the hard-pressed, and they knew how to capitalize upon these frustrations by emphasizing the problems without providing solutions.

Most of the southern demagogues were Populists, members of a political party organized late in the nineteenth century to represent agrarian interests and advocate governmental control of monopolies. Often Populist spokesmen expressed hate for capital investors. Unfortunately, the agrarian interests of the South during this period, particularly in the Deep South, were limited almost exclusively to cotton. As stated earlier, cotton could be counted as both a curse and a blessing but more often as a curse than as a blessing. Cotton drained the land of its rich plant food and made it poorer. It required cheap labor. Generally the people who produced it lived lives of servitude. The cotton laborers worked from sun-up to sun-down. Agrarian reform was a subject about which the demagogues ranted. But little could be done to reform the poverty-perpetuating, one-crop cotton economy until technology devised the means for replacing personal labor and hand tools with more sophisticated equipment. Even then, cotton producers would have to be more selective than they had been in choosing the land to be used for growing cotton. The demagogues could do nothing about developing the essential technology and the sophisticated equipment, selecting the land, nor eliminating slave-type labor, because the price of cotton was determined on the world market and the South was competing with cheap labor around the world. Instead of advocating crop diversification and encouraging the investment of outside capital and the industrialization of the region, the demagogues discouraged capital investment, lambasted Wall Street and an assortment of alleged "trusts," and sought to perpetuate the cheap labor which kept both the white and the black man in servitude.

In *The Mind of the South*, W. J. Cash wrote:

> I think the demagogues would have appeared if Populism and economic and social irritations had never been heard of. A people long fed on strong meat infallibly grows to demand stronger and stronger meat still. And in the South it was unavoidable that a time should come when the best efforts even of the captains of Reconstruction and their direct heirs would no longer seem wholly adequate. For these captains were generally in some ponderable degree under the influence of the aristocratic notion. And in their most extravagant appeals to sectional or Negro hate there was generally something of that uneasiness of conscience over the possible consequences which had all along belonged to the better sort of South-

erner, and so some element of restraint. But restraint would come more and more to be the last thing that the masses of Southerners, including many men who belonged in point of wealth and power to the upper orders, and untroubled by scruples or fears for the outcome of unbridled hate, wanted.[17]

It would be impractical to give a detailed report on all of the demagogues responsible for the high cost the people paid for the products of bad leadership—the thwarted progress, the delayed growth, the years of servitude, the perpetuation of poverty, the exodus of young leadership, the mass injustice, and the creation of a philosophy of backwardness which handicapped millions of people through the years. These demagogues usually were positive in expression and negative in action. They played so dramatically on the passions and prejudices of the people that leaders with positive thinking and potential solutions to problems were silenced and even ridiculed. Thus was created a historic gap between the Deep South and the rest of the nation, particularly an economic and educational gap. This tragic gap remains today. The philosophy of backwardness made the Deep South provincial in viewpoint. The region stood aloof from the rest of the nation and became distrustful of the mainstream of American life.

To emphasize the price the Deep South paid for this drama of the demagogues—the price of this political entertainment—one demagogue has been selected for a detailed discussion. Theodore G. Bilbo, in his early days in the state senate studied the Populist theories of Tom Heflin of

Alabama and "Pitchfork Ben" Tillman of South Carolina. He was a disciple of the "Great White Chief" James K. Vardaman.

NOTES TO CHAPTER 5

[1] Reinhart Luthin, *American Demagogues* (Boston: Beacon Press, 1954), 13.
[2] W. J. Cash, *The Mind of the South* (New York: Random House, 1960), 253.
[3] Luthin, *American Demagogues*, 46–47.
[4] Greenwood (Miss.) *Commonwealth*, August 26, 1897.
[5] *Ibid.*, December 6, 1901.
[6] Albert D. Kirwan, *Revolt of the Rednecks* (Lexington: University of Kentucky Press, 1951), 163.
[7] Natchez *Democrat*, July 4, 1901.
[8] Kirwan, *Revolt of the Rednecks*, 164.
[9] Luthin, *American Demagogues*, 162.   [10] *Ibid.*   [11] *Ibid.*, 262.
[12] Allan A. Michie and Frank Ryhlick, *Dixie Demagogues* (New York: Vanguard Press, 1939), 108.
[13] Luthin, *American Demagogues*, 253.
[14] *Dictionary of American Biography*, XVI, 547.
[15] Luthin, *American Demagogues*, 182.
[16] Michie and Ryhlick, *Dixie Demagogues*, 142.
[17] Cash, *Mind of the South*, 252–53.

6 Russian Roulette

MY PURPOSE HERE is not to compile a record of the official and unofficial acts of Theodore Gilmore Bilbo. More capable men than I have already done this task. Conversely, the objective of this effort is to reveal how the conduct of one demagogue could effect the destiny of the people of a large section of our country. What he did is not here important but the effects of his actions are vital to this story.

Theodore Gilmore (the Man) Bilbo, one of seven children of poor but respected parents, was born October 13, 1877, down in the "gopher country" of Mississippi, so-called not for the fur-bearing type of gopher but the reptile type which has all of the characteristics of a large turtle about the size of a small zinc washtub. His birthplace was a log cabin in Pearl River County, Mississippi, in the tranquil rural community of Juniper Grove.[1]*

Thirty days later, on November 12, 1877, Frederick Sullens was born in Versailles, Missouri. Sullens and Bilbo were destined to perpetuate an extended feud, a marathon of hostility which would be a rough-and-tumble, knock-down, drag-out war of sarcasm, satire, and superlatives between a vitriolic editor and a loquacious political demagogue.[2]

* Notes appear at end of chapter.

The young Bilbo, five feet two, a "scrub oak of a man" with a large skull, jug ears, and a scrappy nature, made his first political race for the office of circuit clerk in Pearl River County against a one-armed Baptist preacher. When the votes were counted Bilbo was defeated by fifty-six votes. "You know," said Bilbo, "I could see that damn empty sleeve when I went into the voting booth." [3]

Four years later, while studying law at Vanderbilt University, he was elected to the state senate and "the man" Bilbo—as he called himself—"the man of the people"—was on his way, a rip-roaring, mud-slinging, political journey of noisy cat-calls, homespun yarns, cutting epithets, and boisterous laughter during symptomatic years which revealed the credulity of the hillbilly folk, their uninhibited gullibility, and their tragic naivete which perpetuated their poverty and developed a philosophy of backwardness which sacrificed their best interests to Bilbo's political domain.

Said Bilbo, "When I walked into that senate chamber for the first session I was not afraid. This was my world and I was going to conquer it."

There is a high ridge called Valley Hill swinging southward from Memphis and extending nearly to Vicksburg which separates the Mississippi hills from the Mississippi Delta. Valley Hill in those years also marked the political division of the state. Perhaps it is significant that the Delta is always capitalized, whereas a lower case H is used to denote the "hills." The Delta people were richer than the hill people, their alluvial soil more fertile, and their cotton plantations larger. Their long staple cotton brought a higher price per pound than that produced elsewhere in the state. Deltans drank more Scotch without sacrificing their quota of Bourbon. In the hills, corn whiskey was the popular drink. The Deltans paid homage to the cultural niceties; the hill folk read their Bibles and prayed reverently. Although the Deltans also read their Bibles, they were not always included in the generalized term "the Bible Belt and Calomel Circle" used to denote the hill country of Mississippi and nearby Alabama. The Delta was the home of the "aristocracy"; the hills, the home of the "rednecks," a term referring less to an overexposure to the hot Mississippi sun than to an underexposure to education. The hill folk distrusted the Deltans, passionately at times, and the Deltans were accused of being contemptuous in their attitude toward the hill folk.

Certain Delta leaders, including the Percys, were more tolerant of Negro people and felt that efforts should be made to educate and encourage them. The hill folk were race-minded primarily as related to white supremacy. This was the stage and Bilbo capitalized upon the stage setting.

Fred Sullens had a penchant for words, an extensive vocabulary, a fighting spirit, and varied moods. He could be romantic, even poetic, and at times humorous; but his newspaper was read more intently when he dipped his pen in venom.

Once in a gentle mood he wrote, "All over Jackson you will find robins hopping over lawns and gardens busily digging for worms. Our American robin is probably our best known bird. It will nest almost anywhere, welcome or not. It will clean more bugs off a lawn than a vacuum cleaner. It will wake its human neighbors with its mating song. It struts like a jaybird. The robin belongs to the thrush family and probably would sing more if it didn't spend so much time feeding itself." [4]

He wrote concerning Colonel Hi Henry, owner of the competing morning daily newspaper: "The colonel became ill and the family physician was summoned. He put the stethoscope to the colonel's chest and said sadly, 'His circulation is just about gone.'" Continued Sullens, "The colonel jumped out of bed and said angrily, 'There's nothing wrong with my circulation. I have 5,000 more circulation than the Jackson *Daily News*.'" [5]

Often Sullens wrote with anger. Referring to a state official, he wrote in his front page column, "The Low Downs on the Higher Ups," "Jim (so-and-so) came to my office today. I beat the hell out of him, and his son, and his dog. If anybody else is looking for trouble, he'll find a well-preserved man in his middle fifties well able to take care of himself." [6]

On December 22, 1909, United States Senator Anselm J. McLaurin of Mississippi died in office. The legislature was responsible for choosing a successor. The race ultimately became a contest between James K. Vardaman—the idol of the "hillbillies," the "Great White Chief," the staunch racist—and Leroy Percy—the corporation lawyer, plantation owner, and Deltan who regarded the black people as human and felt that they should be treated as such.[7]

After the eighty-seven to eighty-two election something happened that had the impact of someone having thrown a high-powered bomb from the legislative gallery to the legislative floor. As described by Albert D. Kirwan, in *Revolt of the Rednecks*, state senator Theodore G. Bilbo announced that he had been approached by two women who told him that money was being paid for Percy votes and urged him to accept some of it. Subsequently he was introduced to a man named Dulaney. Bilbo stated he was promised $500 if he would switch his vote from Vardaman to Percy and an additional $500 if Percy were elected. The matter dragged along, and Dulaney, Bilbo declared, approached him again in Dulaney's room in the Edwards Hotel. At one of these meetings, Bilbo said Dulaney gave him $150; at another, $145. On the day after the election, Bilbo said he had received $350 additional money.[8] Bilbo declared he had accepted the money in order to trap the bribers. Kirwan reported that "Representative Anderson, a teller, stated that he saw Bilbo's ballot on the last vote and that it was marked for Vardaman." [9]

On March 28, 1910, a grand jury indicted Dulaney, a levee contractor of Issaquena County, charging him with paying Bilbo $645 to obtain his vote for Percy. Since the evidence was not decisive, Dulaney was acquitted.[10] In the meantime two legislative investigations were ordered. The Joint Committee on Contingent Funds was instructed to investigate Vardaman's accounts while he was governor. The Senate Committee as a whole was instructed to investigate the bribery charges.[11]

The testimony of an octoroon madam of the "fanciest bordel" in Jackson helped to prove Dulaney's innocence. Unexplained, however, was the testimony of a United

States Treasury official who swore that the "marked bills" Bilbo produced came from an issue not yet released to the banks on the day he claimed to have received them.[12]

On April 14, 1910, when the senate investigation was nearly completed an effort was made to expel Bilbo from the senate. Predictions were that he would be ousted by a vote of twenty-six to thirteen. Ultimately the vote was twenty-eight to fifteen, one vote short of the necessary two thirds required for expulsion of a member.[13]

The senate, by now concerned and disgusted, considered a resolution of condemnation of Bilbo. It read:

> Resolved, in view of the unexplained inconsistencies and inherent improbabilities, in the testimony of Sen. Bilbo, his established bad character and lack of credibility, that the senate of Mississippi, does hereby condemn his entire bribery charge, and the statement of the role he played as detective and decoy, as a trumped up falsehood, utterly unworthy of belief; resolved further, that as a result of the conduct of Theodore G. Bilbo in this matter, and the testimony produced in this investigation, the senate pronounces Bilbo as unfit to sit with honest upright men in a respectable legislative body, and he is hereby asked to resign.[14]

Wrote Fred Sullens in the *Daily News,* "The best thing to do with Bilbo would be to confine him to a small room with a dozen polecats until they stink each other to death." [15]

Two days after the senate adopted the resolution discrediting Bilbo, Leroy Percy made a denunciatory address in which he described Bilbo as a "characterless man, a self-confessed liar, a self-accused bribe-taker, a moral leper."

William Alexander Percy in *Lanterns on the Levee* said that Bilbo was a:

> pert little monster, glib and shameless, with that sort of cunning common to criminals which passes for intelligence. The people loved him. They loved him not because they were deceived in him, but because they understood him thoroughly; they said of him proudly, "He's a slick little bastard." He was one of them and he had risen from obscurity to the fame of glittering infamy—it was as if they themselves had crashed the headlines. Vardaman's glamour waved and this man rode to power. . . . They were the sort of people that . . . mistake hoodlumism for wit, and cunning for intelligence, that attend revivals and fight and fornicate in the bushes afterwards.[16]

Meanwhile Bilbo, the five-foot, two-inch runt of his family, was fighting back. He referred to one of his political adversaries as "the offspring of a hyena and a mongrel, begotten in a graveyard at midnight, suckled by a sow and educated by a damn fool." Outraged, the opponent pistol-whipped him, inflicting facial scars that remained with him for life.[17] During one of these knock-down, drag-out affairs a frenzied Bilboite yelled out, "Hit him Bilbo. Amen. Hallelujah, God Damn."[18] Other encounters resulted. Bilbo called W. D. Gibbs, who had voted for Bilbo's expulsion from the state senate, "a renegade Confederate soldier." "Old Wash Gibbs," as he was called, broke a gold-headed cane over Bilbo's head, knocking him out cold and into a gutter.[19] After this incident Yazoo

City friends presented Gibbs with a new gold-headed cane inscribed "To W. D. Gibbs for one broken on Bilbo's head." [20]

With such a record of confusion and conflict, the average politican would be as dead as a dried mackerel. But Bilbo capitalized on all of the degrading things said about him, announced his candidacy for lieutenant governor, and was elected. The significant question: did this Bilbo victory reflect a resourceful and astute politician? Or did it emphasize the philosophy of backwardness which was so closely tied to the topographical plowing of cotton rows around pine stumps in the hills, a system born in slavery which perpetuated servitude for whites and blacks long after the slaves had been emancipated?

Bilbo was accused of bribery a second time in 1913 when a bill was dropped into the legislative hopper to create a new county in the Delta. The idea behind the venture was to tear apart Washington County, whose residents had opposed him in his race for lieutenant governor. Furthermore, Washington County was the "Percy County." At first the idea was to give the new county the name "Delta." [21] But an amendment was introduced to name it "Vardaman County," a blow proposed to avenge the Percy group by paying homage to the Vardaman-Bilbo faction. Parts of Holmes, Yazoo, Washington, and Leflore counties were to be used to create "Vardaman County."

Earl Brewer, the governor, was hostile to Bilbo. The people of Belzoni, Mississippi, raised a sum of two thousand dollars to promote the new county and placed this money in the hands of Steve Castleman, who was an acquaintance of G. A. Hobbs, in some ways an associate of Bilbo. Suspicions were aroused as to how the money was being used to promote the new county. On December 2, 1913, Bilbo and Hobbs were jointly indicted. Hobbs was charged with having received two hundred dollars. Castleman allegedly swore he gave Hobbs two hundred dollars as part payment on a bribe of two thousand.[22]

Bilbo, the lieutenant governor, and Governor Earl Brewer, his chief, were at loggerheads throughout the administration. On July 10, 1914, after the alleged acceptance of the bribe by Hobbs, Bilbo was acquitted. The defense attorneys, Jim Cassidy and Judge Pat Henry, reputed to be among the most astute criminal lawyers in the state, were in charge of the defense.[23] Despite this record Bilbo was elected governor. Frederick Sullens said, "The great golden eagle on the capitol dome should be replaced by a puking buzzard." [24]

The Man Bilbo, in turn, was succeeded by Governor Lee Russell, his personal and political friend. A seduction suit was brought against Russell. Involved was litigation seeking $100,000 involving an alleged breach of promise. Bilbo was sought as a witness but he did not want to testify. Wigfall Green wrote in *The Man Bilbo* that Bilbo admitted, and the girl agreed, that he, acting as attorney for Russell, had given her $250. Russell suddenly shifted position and charged that Bilbo had instigated action to harass him, whereupon Bilbo was summoned as a witness. So he avoided the courts.[25]

A subpoena was issued for Bilbo's appearance. When he failed to respond Judge Edwin R. Holmes found him in contempt of court, fined him a hundred dollars, and sentenced him to thirty days in the Oxford, Mississippi, jail. The sentence was later reduced to ten days.[26]

Fred Sullens wrote that the deputy had searched diligently for Bilbo and was about to give up when he heard a heifer calf bawl in a barn. He decided to investigate and found Bilbo in a stall with the heifer calf. Continued Sullens, "Some people sympathize with Governor Russell. Some sympathize with the girl. Some give their sympathy to Bilbo. But personally all of our sympathy goes to the heifer calf." [27]

Obviously Bilbo was not only in jail but in the headlines as well, and he made the most of it. From the jail he announced his candidacy for a second term for governor. The jail sentence almost took on characteristics of a vacation. Bilbo was allowed to entertain visitors, was served meals from the university, was treated as if he were an honored guest.

Uninhibited and unabashed, Bilbo promised one plank in his platform for each day of his confinement. But when the campaign was staged, he was defeated by Henry Whitfield, president of a state girls' college. But the vote was significant: Whitfield, 134,715; Bilbo, 118,143.[28]

Four years later Bilbo again sought a second term as governor. He promised to build a great system of highways for the state, saying that Mississippi had an excess of convict labor and an abundance of red clay. He advocated floating a bond issue of $60 million with which to build a state brick plant to manufacture vitrified brick and to build highways with convict labor. He said, "My countrymen, we can lay these vitrified bricks on one side and use them for 100 years. Then we can turn them over and use them for another hundred years. And then we can stand them on end and use them right up to Kingdom come."

Bilbo also advocated the establishment of a state printing plant because the hard-pressed farmers found it burdensome to buy textbooks for their children. Advocates of the plan declared that money could be saved by having the state print schoolbooks for the children. The Mississippi Press Association actively opposed the idea of the proposed state printing plant. Because I was president of the Mississippi Press Association at that time I became involved in the controversy. I asked Bilbo, "Who will write our textbooks should the state decide to print them?" He replied, "We have able men and women in our state. We can capitalize on the educational talent of our own people. We'll write our own textbooks."

This time Bilbo was elected by a landslide. He went into office angry at the college professors who had helped to defeat him four years before. To obtain jobs for patronage and revenge for his earlier defeat, Bilbo dismissed 179 college faculty members. Their offense was that they had tried to rid the state of demagoguery and four years earlier had supported Henry Whitfield, the college president. Bilbo did not take defeat lightly. He demanded revenge.[29]

John B. Hudson wrote in the *New Republic:*

> Theodore G. Bilbo, five feet two, scarred in the face by a pistol butt, an ex-bribe taker, Baptist preacher, lawyer, country school teacher, swaggered out of a meeting of

the board of trustees of the state university and colleges to greet waiting reporters. "Boys," he said, with a ring of pride in his voice, "We've just hung up a new record. We've bounced three college presidents and made three new ones in the record time of two hours. "And," continued the governor, adjusting his diamond horseshoe pin and his flaming red necktie, "that's just the beginning of what's going to happen." [30]

Of the three hundred first-year students enrolled at the University of Mississippi just before Bilbo's spoils system went into effect, all but 109 withdrew.[31]

President Hugh Critz of A&M College, one of Bilbo's new appointees, commented to some of his associates, "I have just been handed a blacklist for A&M College which contains the names of those faculty members who are to be dismissed. Many of them are my friends and are highly trained in their professions and I do not see how they are going to be replaced. I am shocked and paralyzed. Indeed, gentlemen, it has sent me through the Garden of Gethsemane." [32]

During the 1930 session of the Southern Association of Colleges and Secondary Schools, four of Mississippi's major institutions of higher learning lost their accreditation as a result of Bilbo's actions. The reason given by the association was the wholesale firing of faculty members without warning, without charges, without the opportunity of defense and without action by the administrative heads of these institutions. Mississippi, in a sense, was exiled from the educational world—excommunicated, so to speak.[33]

Chancellor J. H. Kirkland of Vanderbilt University

called the action of Bilbo and the board of trustees "the most notorious and disgraceful act in the history of American education." Bilbo replied, "Things have come to a hell of a pass when a fellow can't wallop his own jackass."

I received a taste of how Bilbo dealt with people who disagreed with him. In those days of deflation my newspaper printed a special bulletin which had been authorized by the legislature. The contract, amounting to about fifteen hundred dollars was let by the state Department of Agriculture and Commerce. The warrant, under the law at that time, required the governor's signature. At the end of the first month after the bill was due, Bilbo wrote, "Please send statement in duplicate." At the end of second month he wrote, "Please send statement in triplicate." At the end of the fourth month he wrote, "Please send statement in quadruplicate." Finally the month of December rolled around. I wrote across the statement. "Merry Christmas, governor—and if my family has a Merry Christmas I'll have to have a state warrant instead of a request for more statements." He replied, "I suppose you have waited long enough for your money. Merry Christmas." The warrant was enclosed.

For fifteen years Bilbo hoarded material with which to build his "dream house" at Juniper Grove, just opposite the log house in which he was born. The columns of the "Old Mansion" were from the old capitol, a building drenched in history. Bilbo, as builder, bought the old columns for a dollar each. But the sale cost him the good will of the United Daughters of the Confederacy.[34]

There were more than one hundred fine walnut panels

in the old state capitol. After suggesting that they be sold at auction, Bilbo bought them for a dollar each. The United Daughters of the Confederacy publicly expressed their resentment and urged him to return them to the state. The Daughters of the American Revolution stated flatly that the transaction was illegal. Despite the turbulent appeal, Bilbo was insensitive to the request and shipped the panels to Poplarville to become a part of his ornate "dream house." Throughout the state speculation was rife as to how the governor, drawing a salary of $7,500, could build a mansion costing upward of $100,000.[35]

One juicy fiasco referred to as the "$80,000 highway scandal" added to the controversy and excitement of the Bilbo regime.[36] It emphasized what Bilbo had said, "The only entertainment the country people have are revivals and politics." So Bilbo, the lay Baptist preacher of Hobolochitto Baptist Association who often opened his speeches with "Hallelujah," made his entertainment dramatic and colorful.

The state mental hospital had 2,500 patients in an institution built to accommodate 1,500. Bilbo held up work on the institution until the architect working on his "dream house" was made associate architect on the state institution at a salary of ten thousand dollars. There were complaints that the architect spent too much time on Bilbo's private project.

The administration was severely condemned for pardoning 634 convicts, many of them murderers serving life sentences.

Because the state treasury was short of funds, members

of the legislature, led by four representatives known as the "Big Four" and headed by Tom Bailey, the House Speaker, asked the governor to call the legislature into special session to cope with emergencies. The governor agreed to call the special session provided a majority of the legislators would sign a non-impeachment pledge. Said Bilbo, "I'll have nothing to do with the fool session. Let them sign the non-impeachment pledge and I'll announce the call in thirty minutes." The session was not held.[37]

In two years Bilbo had raised the state debt from $28,708,000 to $50,006,500.[38] When Bilbo left office his successor found a total of $1,326.17 in the state treasury.[39] The first act of Governor Mike Conner, Bilbo's successor, was to give his personal check to provide food for patients at the Mississippi Mental Hospital at Whitfield. The state's credit was exhausted.[40] And the year Bilbo went out of the governor's office, the per capita income of Mississippi was $126.00.[41]

I well remember that my mother-in-law asked my wife, "Why does your husband dislike Bilbo?" I had made the statement that I had never voted for Bilbo and never would. That made me some kind of a sinner, an oddball, a quack, someone out of touch with the realities of the struggling common man.

When the catcalls were silenced and the wild yelling quieted down, one thing was obvious: the game the excited crowds had been playing was Russian roulette.

In 1944 I was named by Governor Tom Bailey to a twelve-year term on the board of trustees of the Mississippi Institutions of Higher Learning. H. H. Crisler, editor of the Port Gibson (Miss.) *Reveille*, published near the campus of Alcorn A&M College, the Negro land-grant college, came to see me. He stated, "I would like to know what your policy will be toward Alcorn." I told him that I was very much concerned with seeing some substantial improvements made in education for black youths in Mississippi. He replied, "I knew this would be your attitude but I wanted you to know that I'm willing to help you if you need me." Then Mr. Crisler made this statement: "Shortly after Bilbo had named his board of trustees I put this same question to one of the board members. He replied, 'I don't give a damn what they do with Alcorn A&M College. As far as I am personally concerned they can put one hundred sticks of dynamite under it and blow it to hell.' " [42]

NOTES TO CHAPTER 6

[1] Louis Cochran, "Mussolini of Mississippi, A Portrait of Governor Bilbo—the Builder," *Outlook*, CLVIII (Fall, 1931), 222-23.

[2] John Ray Skates, "The Sullens-Bilbo Feud," *Collegere*, I (Spring, 1965), 4-7.

[3] "Probes: Bilbo's Lovely Dreams," *Newsweek*, December 30, 1946, pp. 18-19.

[4] Jackson (Miss.) *Daily News*, October 10, 1954. This was one of the paragraphs selected by the *Daily News* staff to be read at the banquet honoring Sullens' fiftieth anniversary as editor.

[5] *Ibid.*   [6] *Ibid.*

[7] A. Wigfall Green, *The Man Bilbo* (Baton Rouge: Louisiana State University Press, 1963), 25.

[8] Albert D. Kirwan, *Revolt of the Rednecks* (Lexington: University of Kentucky Press, 1951), 199.

[9] *Ibid.*, 200.   [10] *Ibid.*, 197.   [11] *Ibid.*, 198-99.

[12] Allan A. Michie and Frank Ryhlick, *Dixie Demagogues* (New York: Vanguard Press, 1939), 93.

[13] *Ibid.*, 34.   [14] *Ibid.*, 94.   [15] *Ibid.*, 47.

[16] William Alexander Percy, *Lanterns on the Levee* (New York: Alfred A. Knopf, 1941), 148-49.
[17] Michie and Ryhlick, *Dixie Demagogues*, 95.
[18] Green, *The Man Bilbo*, 39.
[19] Jackson (Miss.) *Daily News*, May 26, 1911.   [20] *Ibid.*
[21] G. A. Hobbs, *Bilbo, Brewer & Bribery in Mississippi Politics* (Jackson, Miss.: Jackson Municipal Library, 1917), 6.
[22] Green, *The Man Bilbo*, 45-57.   [23] *Ibid.*   [24] *Ibid.*, 69.
[25] Memphis *News Scimitar*, June 23, 1930.
[26] John B. Hudson, "The Spoils System Enters College," *New Republic*, LXIV (September 17, 1930), 123-25.
[27] Jackson (Miss.) *Daily News*, October 10, 1954.
[28] Green, *The Man Bilbo*, 69.
[29] Clarence E. Cason, "The Mississippi Imbroglio," *Virginia Quarterly Review*, VII (April, 1931), 238.
[30] Hudson, "Spoils System," 123.   [31] *Ibid.*, 125.   [32] *Ibid.*, 123.
[33] Minutes of a meeting of the board of trustees, Mississippi Institutions of Higher Learning, III, 278-79.
[34] Jackson (Miss.) *Daily News*, June 15, 1967.   [35] *Ibid.*
[36] Memphis *Commercial Appeal*, March 1, 1931.
[37] Reinhart Luthin, *American Demagogues* (Boston: Beacon Press, 1954), 13.
[38] Mississippi Journal of the House of Representatives (1932), 324.
[39] Jackson (Miss.) *Daily News*, January 21, 1932.
[40] Frank Wallace, "A History of the Conner Administration" (M. A. thesis, Mississippi College, 1959), 20.
[41] U. S. Department of Commerce, Office of Business Economics, *Survey on Current Business* (1956), 142. See also supplement, "Personal Income by States," 1929.
[42] Conversation with author, Port Gibson, Mississippi, June 5, 1940.

7 Fetter in Washington

THIS IS NOT a biography of the "Stormy Petrel." If it were, I would be obligated to detail the progressive legislation he sponsored. What is written here is the substance of his career in Washington, his sense of direction, and particularly the direction in which the people of the Deep South moved under his leadership. Don't question it. He led them. Also observed here is Bilbo's pattern of operation and how this pattern affected the people. Did he challenge people to think, to grow, to reach for nobler and finer things? The contrary is true.

Actually, Bilbo's thoughts and his pattern of operation, along with the thoughts and pattern of conduct of other Deep South demagogues, influenced the thinking and the behavior of a majority of the people of the Deep South. Those who were not consciously inclined to embrace this thinking and this behavior were subconsciously motivated by both because this behavior became a way of life which included a divorce from reality, marriage to the status quo, a belief that the rest of America was hostile to the region, a demand for conformity, and a grave fear of the future. These fallacious beliefs kept the Deep South out of the mainstream of American life and created an educational, spiritual, and economic gap. This gap was accompanied by a much lower per capita income than the national average and caused many educated young men and women to become disenchanted and move to other areas in search of opportunities not available in this region. This exodus of bright young minds was, and still is, hurtful; and the gap has not yet been closed.

Until just a few years ago the economic status of the Deep South was closely akin to that of the have-not nations of Latin America.[1]* Nevertheless, instead of working together and meeting basic problems head-on, the people were guffawing at wisecracks shouted from the political stump. Bilbo, the demagogue here chosen to reveal the waste created by demagogues generally in this region, pegged his political hopes on a simple though startling formula. Milton Lehman wrote in the *Saturday Evening Post*, "First you must provide the voters with enemies, real or imaginary, and slam them; second, you must scream 'martyrdom' loud enough so the voters will come to your support."

Deep South leaders who tried to alter this semi-primitive way of life in an effort to close the economic gap have been severely criticized because of their nonconformity. Reason often was interpreted as treason.

In January, 1932, when he was succeeded by Governor Mike Conner, Bilbo joined the army of unemployed. He went to Washington to see Senator Pat Harrison in an effort to land a job. Pat Harrison was in a willing mood because he wanted to get Bilbo out of Mississippi. So Bilbo was given a six thousand dollar a year job clipping newspapers for the Agricultural Adjustment Administration.[2]

* Notes appear at end of chapter.

"By the way, Pat," Bilbo commented as he was leaving Senator Harrison's office, "some of my friends want me to run for the senate next year." [3]

"Well, well," replied the senator, "I hadn't heard that."

Within a short time, however, when Bilbo began to hold press conferences, Senator Harrison decided Washington was not far enough away from Mississippi for Bilbo. Shortly thereafter he suggested to Bilbo that he could render distinctive public service by accepting a position as sugar inspector in the Philippines.[4]

About this time Sullens concocted a new title for Bilbo and was publicizing him as the "Pastemaster General of the United States." Resenting the ridicule and much chagrined and angered, Bilbo resigned his post, returned to Mississippi in 1933, and ran against Senator Hubert Stephens the following year.[5]

Bilbo knew that he was confronted with the opposition of Senator Harrison. Before leaving Washington, he called on the senator and said, "Pat, I'm going to run on a theory. The theory is that you want Stephens elected because so long as he's in Washington you have two votes in your pocket. And you don't want me to run because you know if I run I'll win and then you'll have only one vote in your pocket. That's what I'm going to tell the people of Mississippi. And if you come down to fight for Stephens it would be the best thing for me. It would confirm my theory." [6]

Bilbo often said, "My name means a two-edged sword and I'm both edges." But there is another definition for the name Bilbo—"a fetter consisting of two sliding shackles attached to an iron bar." The question then arose: would Bilbo be a fetter in Washington? Would his pattern of political behavior be the same in Washington as it was in Mississippi? Would Washington respond to his P. T. Barnum tactics as did the roaring hillbillies in Mississippi?

The tempo of Bilbo's campaign was emphasized in the way he characterized his opponent Senator Hubert Stephens. From the stump Bilbo declared, "He is a vicious, malicious, pusillanimous, cold-blooded, premediated, plain, ordinary, United States liar." [7] Obviously Senator Stephens could not meet all these conditions as a chronic purveyor of untruths because he could not be a plain, ordinary liar if Bilbo's full description applied. In the campaign Bilbo quoted some lines from Huey P. Long, the demagogue from Louisiana. He shouted from the stump, "In the scheme of this government it was intended that every man be a king and every woman a queen."

The election resulted in Bilbo's receiving 102,078 votes; Stephens, 94,991—a close victory margin of 7,087.[8]

The tone of the campaign indicated that Bilbo and Huey Long might get together in the United States Senate. The two would have made a powerful political team. But the natures of the two men and their patterns of operation were too similar. Bilbo, the "Man," the "Stormy Petrel" with the flashing red necktie, the red galluses, and the diamond horseshoe stickpin, envied Huey Long, the "Kingfish," the "Comic Opera Star," the "Bonaparte of the Bayous," "Der Fuhrer of Louisiana." Each was a prima donna. Each had to command the center of the stage.

Neither could share the spotlight. Inevitably a feud developed between them.

Two months after Bilbo was sworn into the Senate he appeared in the cloakroom with his right eye blackened and a bandaged wound on the left side of his massive head. Nearby Long appeared with a bandaged left hand. Some senator asked Huey, "Did you get that bandage by leading with your left to Bilbo's eye?" The Kingfish replied, "Oh, no. I've got a case of athelete's foot in my hand." [9]

In a radio address in New Orleans Long boasted that he had given Bilbo the margin of victory in his Senate campaign and shouted, "The low down rat went to Washington, got a few jobs and said he was 'anti Long.' " Bilbo had no opportunity to reply because just two days later Long was cut down by an assassin's bullet at the State Capitol in Baton Rouge.[10]

Bilbo and Harrison continued at loggerheads. Senator Harrison became a candidate for the Senate Democratic majority leader. His opponent was the jovial Senate storyteller, Senator Alben Barkley of Kentucky. Senator Bilbo sent word to Harrison that he would vote for his colleague if Harrison would ask him to do so. When told of Bilbo's offer, Harrison replied, "I wouldn't speak to that son-of-a-bitch if it meant the Presidency of the United States." When the votes were counted the result was a victory for Barkley, thirty-eight to thirty-seven.[11]

Bilbo's lust for revenge went with him to the United States Senate. President Franklin Roosevelt appointed Judge Edwin R. Holmes of Mississippi to a federal judgeship. Judge Holmes had sentenced Bilbo to a term in the Oxford, Mississippi, jail for contempt in the Russell seduction case during the early years of Bilbo's career. Harrison led the fight for Judge Holmes' confirmation. But not Bilbo. He got possession of the Senate floor and for two hours bitterly assailed Judge Holmes for his contempt and his ignorance in remanding him to jail. Judge Holmes' appointment was, nevertheless, confirmed.[12]

In June, 1938, Bilbo, recognizing that the time was approaching for his second-term race, caught the ear of the nation with his "back-to-Africa" campaign. He first sought an amendment to the Senate Works Relief Bill which he claimed would send twelve million blacks back to Africa, solve the problem of unemployment, and reduce racial tensions.[13]

Mrs. Eleanor Roosevelt opposed the "Back-to-Africa" idea. Said Bilbo, "If I can succeed in resettling the great majority of the Negroes in West Africa—and I propose to do it—I might entertain the proposition of crowning Eleanor Roosevelt queen of Greater Liberia." [14]

The senator proposed to establish a greater Liberia by wangling 400,000 square miles of an area adjacent to Liberia from Great Britain and France as part payment of their war debts. The United States was to subsidize the project, but blacks were to go to Africa of their own free will. He claimed that a petition circulated by a mulatto in Chicago bore the names of 2,500,000 persons who wanted to go to Africa. Asked who would pick the cotton, Bilbo replied, "The mechanical cotton picker—and it won't be demanding social equality or intermarriage with the whites." [15]

The "Back-to-Africa" effort brought Bilbo under severe

attack from both senators and representatives, many of whom made capital of it. They attacked Bilbo and the people of the Deep South. Bilbo relayed the attacks to his own constituents, who in turn became angry and defiant. Their own anger and defiance of outside interference drew them closer to Bilbo. He withdrew his amendment and confessed it was but a gesture for publicity. Then on April 24, 1939, he again launched his program, this time as a regular Senate bill. He utilized twenty-six pages in the *Congressional Record*, reputedly at a cost to the government of $50 per page, to explain his Back-to-Africa program. He called upon the federal government to provide one billion dollars to finance a Negro nation in Africa.[16]

Bilbo's scheme brought attacks upon him and his state from all sides. Obviously the Back-to-Africa movement was resented, particularly in those states with politically potent blacks in large numbers. When politicians in such areas retaliated in harsh words, Bilbo matched them in the exchange of venom. He spoke out against the "nigger-loving Damn Yankees" with the inevitable result that the people sent Bilbo back for a second term with a wide winning margin.[17]

President Harry Truman became Bilbo's new target of attack. The president advanced a civil rights program to aid the black people. The program included a federal anti-lynching bill, an anti-poll tax bill, a federal Fair Employment Act, and a proposal to eliminate racial discrimination in the armed services.[18] Bilbo charged that Truman was trying to discredit his state's constitution of 1890 which made it illegal for a black person to vote.

Bilbo caught the attention of the nation when he staged a filibuster against Truman's proposed federal anti-lynching law, a law purposed to bring an end to lynching in the United States. At home he also denounced the "nigger lovers of the senate." He attacked the proposed Fair Employment Practices Act which he said would prohibit discrimination against Negroes in the matter of jobs. He claimed this proposal was aimed directly against his own people.[19]

Meanwhile the Mississippi senator became involved in the race for mayor of New York when the candidate from the black belt of Harlem demanded that the two New York senators seek to have Bilbo ousted from the United States Senate.

Life published the result of the Washington news correspondents' poll which named Bilbo as the "worst man in the senate." [20]

Senator Robert Taft of Ohio charged that Bilbo was a "disgrace to the Senate"—the same charge a majority of state senators in Mississippi had voted several years before when Bilbo was saved from impeachment by only one vote —which meant one vote less than two thirds of the Senate.[21]

Despite all these attacks, Bilbo returned to his home base, ran for a third term, and carried seventy-six of Mississippi's eighty-two counties.[22] Then big trouble commenced to pile up around him.

The campaign which Bilbo had waged for his third term had been carefully scrutinized and discussed in Washington. Senator Robert Taft said, "There is no excuse for him," and "He's a disgrace to the Senate." Bilbo responded,

"As for Mr. Taft we know him in the Senate as Mr. Blah-Blah-Blah. When I think of him, I think of a young mockingbird, just hatched out of his shell, all mouth and no bird at all." [23]

Bilbo's flippancy and his disregard for ethics forced him into a critical position. In December, 1946, a Campaign Investigating Committee held a public hearing in Jackson, Mississippi. Many blacks just home from World War II had been taught in the armed services to participate in civic matters. They went to the public committee hearing.[24] More than 150 of them came to the meeting to testify. They recalled how Bilbo had resorted to innuendo during the campaign when he said, "You and I know the best way to keep the nigger from voting. You do it the night before the election. I don't have to tell you more." [25] One black testified that Bilbo's speech made him afraid to register, another that he had been brutally beaten and warned not to vote. Two said they were told to stay away from the polls. A white priest and a white rabbi complained of the fear resulting from Bilbo's oratory.[26]

Gerald K. Smith, mentioned as one of the demagogues of depression days, launched a national crusade set out with the support of Bilbo. Searching for a cause he settled on that old standby for aspiring dictators—anti-Semitism. Bilbo had to keep his name before the people. He hated most to be ignored by the press.[27]

Meanwhile the Senate War Investigating Committee under the chairmanship of Senator James Mead of New York was investigating Bilbo. The committee was checking into the relationships between Bilbo and war contractors.

FETTER IN WASHINGTON

Senator Mead, on opening the hearing, read the law which prohibited political candidates from soliciting funds from government contractors.[28] A. Wigfall Green, who has written an excellent biography of Bilbo, relates, "Beginning with small skeins, the investigators slowly wove a heavy rope about Bilbo's neck."[29] One of five contractors had given Bilbo a Cadillac as a Christmas gift. Such a gift, Bilbo said, was "just an old southern custom." The same contractor allegedly used his machinery to help Bilbo build a lake and a swimming pool at his "dream house." The cost, nearly four thousand dollars, had allegedly been inadvertently charged to the Keesler Air Field Base account. Another contractor who had sold a half million dollars in building materials to the government covered the "dream house" swimming pool.[30] Many other irregularities were revealed. Bilbo said, "Christ had his Judas Iscariot; Caesar had his Brutus; George Washington had his Benedict Arnold. But I claim to have had the greatest of them all in my trusted secretary."[31] A majority of the Senate War Investigating Committee approved a severe report on Bilbo. It was a definite setback for him.

Tragically, his world seemed to tumble down all around Bilbo with an amazing suddenness. He had developed cancer of the throat.[32]

On January 3, 1947, newly elected senators were to be sworn into office. The first was Raymond E. Baldwin of Connecticut, followed by Theodore G. Bilbo on his third time around. Baldwin was sworn in. Bilbo was next in line. These were tense and historical moments. Bilbo a sick man, was game and cocky, but he was no doubt embarrassed.[33]

Some senators were determined to stop him at the Senate door. Others from the South, knowing the feeling of their people, were determined to have him seated. The Mississippi governor stated that if Bilbo were denied a seat he would appoint him as the successor.

Originally the plan was to bar "Bilbo at the Senate door until the Senate could be organized." The Senate could then debate Bilbo's qualifications. Unexpectedly, Senator Glen Taylor from Idaho, a "onetime tent show player and singing cowboy," got the floor and spoke for an hour opposing the seating of Bilbo who observed, "The greatest joke is that this nincompoop, this cowboy named Taylor, stole the whole Republican show." [34]

Behind closed doors the senators finally agreed to delay the seating of Bilbo until his health would permit him to defend himself. In the meanwhile, he would draw his salary as a United States senator. Senator Alben Barkley had moved, and consent was unanimously granted that in view of his present physical condition the credentials of Bilbo lie on the table without prejudice and without action "until the attending physician at the Capitol shall certify that Mr. Bilbo is able to be in the Senate." [35]

The following day, January 4, 1947, Bilbo bowed out of the United States Senate. He got into his Cadillac to drive to Mississippi, his imposing "dream house," his home. "If I live," he said as he left Washington, "the people of Mississippi will send me back. If I don't live, it doesn't matter either way." He then went to Touro Infirmary in New Orleans for further surgery and medication.[36]

Two months later, in March, Bilbo decided to host a

feast for his Baptist friends at the dedication of the new Juniper Grove Church. Ten thousand persons attended. "When it comes to being a Baptist," he said, "I'm as strong as horseradish." [37] This remark recalled a situation early in his career when a crowd had gathered outside a small Baptist church. Someone said, "He's as good in the pulpit as he is on the stump." Bilbo was in the crowd and he was invited to help with the church program. The short little fellow with the big skull and thin lips sat down before the small church organ and played and sang, "Lord lift me up and let me stand, by faith on heaven's tableland. A higher plane than I have found. Lord plant my feet on higher ground." The point was well made.

W. F. Bond, respected leader in the educational realm during the Bilbo years, recalled that in a conversation with Bilbo the senator expressed a strong dislike for Senator Taft and added that he planned to "jump on" Senator Huey Long in the senate cloak room because of Long's attitude toward President Franklin Roosevelt. Not long after this conversation, death had claimed all three of these men. Bilbo and Taft were both victims of cancer; Long of an assassin's bullet. Bilbo is buried in a mausoleum in the shadow of his beloved "dream house," Long in the shadow of the beautiful new capitol he built for his native state, and Taft in Indian Hill Cemetery in Cincinnati, the city of his birth.[38] Mr. Bond commented further, "As someone quoting from Shakespeare's *Macbeth* said, after viewing the graves of Mary, Queen of Scots, and Queen Elizabeth, 'After life's fitful fever they sleep well.'" [39]

On June 6, 1967, there was an added touch of sadness

to the Bilbo story. The Jackson *Daily News* published the following account:

> Poplarville, Miss. (Special) The highly publicized "Dream House" of the controversial late Mississippi governor Theodore G. Bilbo was destroyed by fire early today. No one was home when fire struck the 26-room, three-story structure that was built by the former Mississippi Governor and United States Senator over a five-year period.[40]

I talked personally with Bilbo on several occasions, and he impressed me as a lonely man. He had a sense of humor and would say things and then chuckle at what he had said. His tragic end aroused emotions that stem from human sympathy. Yet sympathy thus extended is not from an understanding of what he did to the state and region but rather from the human emotion to forgive and forget.

In those final days, after Bilbo had been sent to Ochsner's Clinic and the issue of his being seated or not being seated had become merely academic in view of his impending death, Fred Sullens wrote:

> Mississippi has not been deprived of her rights by what happened in Washington. The unfavorable publicity the state has received from the washing of dirty linen in Washington was well deserved—a proper punishment for having re-elected Bilbo in face of the charges preferred against him. Some day perhaps sober judgment and common sense will convince the people of Mississippi that Bilbo should never have been elected to any office.[41]

NOTES TO CHAPTER 7

[1] U. S. Department of Commerce, Office of Business Economics, *Survey on Current Business* (1956), 142. See also supplement, "Personal Income by States," 1929.
[2] New York *Times*, December 22, 1946.
[3] Jackson (Miss.) *Clarion Ledger-Daily News*, October 6, 1963.
[4] *Ibid.*
[5] Reinhart Luthin, *American Demagogues* (Boston: Beacon Press, 1954), 100.
[6] Allan A. Michie and Frank Ryhlick, *Dixie Demagogues* (New York: Vanguard Press, 1939), 101.
[7] Luthin, *American Demagogues*, 63. [8] *Ibid.*, 64.
[9] Memphis *Commercial Appeal*, February 22, 1935.
[10] Luthin, *American Demagogues*, 65.
[11] New York *Times*, July 21, 1937.
[12] Luthin, *American Demagogues*, 66. [13] *Ibid.*, 68.
[14] *Congressional Record*, 78th Congress, 1944, p. 6253.
[15] Luthin, *American Demagogues*, 68.
[16] Michie and Ryhlick, *Dixie Demagogues*, 105; see also *83rd Congressional Record*, February 1, 1938, pp. 1341-1347; February 2, 1938, pp. 1389-1399; February 7, 1938, pp. 1533-1563.
[17] Luthin, *American Demagogues*, 69.
[18] *81st Congressional Record*, April 19, 1937, p. 3575.
[19] Luthin, *American Demagogues*, 69. [20] *Ibid.*, 70.
[21] New York *Times*, December 22, 1946.
[22] Luthin, *American Demagogues*, 72.
[23] A. Wigfall Green, *The Man Bilbo* (Baton Rouge: Louisiana State University Press, 1963), 110.
[24] Luthin, *American Demagogues*, 73.
[25] *Ibid.*, 71; see also *93rd Congressional Record*, January 3, 1947, p. 76.
[26] New York *Times*, December 2-16, 1946.
[27] David H. Bennett, *Demagogues in the Depression* (New Brunswick, N.J.: Rutgers University Press, 1969), 285.
[28] New York *Times*, December 12-19, 1946; see also *93rd Congressional Record*, January 4, 1947, pp. 83-108.
[29] Green, *The Man Bilbo*, 111. [30] *Time*, December 20, 1946.
[31] *Newsweek*, December 12, 1946.
[32] New York *Times*, September 1, 1946.
[33] Green, *The Man Bilbo*, 116.
[34] *Time*, January 13, 1947; see also *93rd Congressional Record*, January 3, 1947, pp. 7-28.
[35] U.S. Senate, *Journal*, 1947, p. 5; see also *93rd Congressional Record*, January 3, 1947, p. 20

36 Luthin, *American Demagogues*, 74.
37 *New York Times*, June 30, 1946.
38 W.F. Bond, *I Had a Friend* (Kansas City, Mo.: E. L. Mendenhall, 1958), 156.
39 *Ibid.*, 157.
40 Jackson (Miss.) *Daily News*, June 6, 1967.   41 *Ibid.*

8 States' Rights Campaign

THE NATIONAL DEMOCRATIC PARTY CONVENTION of 1948 met in Philadelphia, Pennsylvania. I walked out of that convention with the other delegates from Mississippi and one half of the delegates from Alabama. But if I could retrace my steps and again be given the opportunity to make this decision, I would not walk out.

Many people believe that the Alabama "rednecks" were responsible for Tom Heflin; that the Louisiana "coonasses" kept Huey Long in power; and that the Mississippi "hillbillies" were the exclusive patrons of Theodore Gilmore Bilbo. This statement is not true. Cottonfield philosophy motivated the political behavior of the most prestigious and responsible leaders of the Deep South.

In the light of history, the states' rights campaign of 1948, can be seen as an outgrowth of the thinking of the rednecks, the coonasses, and the hillbillies. But it was acceptable to the political elite as well. An analysis of the philosophy of the cottonfield reveals the reason for this strange political solidification.

Although Bilbo was no longer on the scene, the philosophy he preached was embraced by the Mississippi delegation in the convention and by the Deep South delegates as a whole. Paradoxically, many of the Mississippi delegates had been vigorously "anti-Bilbo" in their politics.

But during this convention, his philosophy—the "cotton field philosophy"—was militantly upheld. It was another instance revealing just how insidious and entrapping this type of thinking could be.

President Harry Truman, then regarded as the political "under-dog," advanced his four-point program in the convention. It was the same program Bilbo had vigorously opposed in the Senate: (1) a federal anti-lynching law, (2) the right of minority groups to vote, (3) a fair employment act, and (4) the elimination of discrimination in the armed services.[1]*

These proposals, all involving race, revived memories of the Reconstruction era, a period of fear, ferment, and frustration when southern whites were disfranchised and the control of government was in the hands of carpet-baggers and newly emancipated blacks. The proposals recalled to mind a time when some form of "Marshall Plan" should have been applied to the South rather than the spirit of revenge, hate, and exploitation as southerners generally interpreted the happenings of that crucial hour in history.

I must admit that I was entrapped by this philosophy. I opposed lynching, believed that minority groups should have the right to vote, felt that the best interests of the economy as well as justice would be served by a fair utilization of Negro employment, and recognized the justification of eliminating discrimination within the armed services. The approach taken to states' rights entrapped me, since I believe in the concept which upholds the constitutional

* Notes appear at end of chapter.

rights of the states. As I now see it, the proposition of constitutional rights was confused. What many persons thought to be constitutional states' rights actually were not constitutional rights at all. During recent years, this point of view has been confirmed by the courts. I believe in constitutional government. To be loyal to the concept of constitutional government one must be willing to pursue constitutional means of determining what is and what is not constitutional. The American way does not permit any man to interpret the Constitution for himself. The Constitution must be changed, if need be, in a constitutional way. Otherwise, there can be but one of two alternatives —accept it or reject it. I choose to accept it.

Governor Fielding Wright and others on the staff of the states' rights movement asked me to devote my full time to the campaign leading to the Philadelphia Convention of the national Democratic party and to a states' rights campaign which late in 1947 was regarded as a certainty. I was to travel with the candidates, ghost-write speeches, and serve as a liaison between the governors of the Deep South states. I agreed.

Shortly after this appointment was announced in the newspapers, Governor Wright received a telegram signed by fourteen citizens of my home bailiwick vigorously protesting my official participation in the campaign and attacking my concepts as revealed in editorials I had written. Governor Wright handed me the telegram, commenting, "You can file this in the wastebasket if you wish. I have no use for it."

For years following my interview with Dr. E. Stanley

Jones I had personally accepted the principle behind the Boston Tea Party and had applied it to the situation in the South. The founding fathers threw that tea from the ship into the sea to make it clear to George III, king of England, that they were opposed to "taxation without representation." This battle cry of the American Revolution was supported by a belligerent patriotism which was too American for me to reject.

Some persons reasoned that franchise for all people would degrade politics. But politics was already degraded in the Deep South, and I reasoned that if politicians were restrained by the voting of all people they would cease to use the Negro as a political "whipping boy." As a result, politics would be upgraded.

The record of lynching in the United States is a sordid one. But contrary to the belief of many people lynching was by no means limited to the Deep South. Charges of lynching were recorded in all but six states. Moreover, the heinous crime of lynching was not limited to black victims: many whites were also lynched. From 1882 to 1947, the year the states' rights organization was founded, 4,735 lynchings occurred in which the victims were murdered primarily by rope or fire. Of the 4,735 lynching victims, 3,432 were black and 1,302 were white—the lynchings occurred in forty-four states.[2] Some states amassed hideous records during this sixty-five year period: Mississippi, 851; Georgia, 531; Louisiana, 391; Alabama, 347; Arkansas, 284. Records in other states revealed: Texas, 493; Montana, 84; Oklahoma, 122; Missouri, 122; West Virginia, 48; Indiana, 47; Ohio, 26; Colorado, 68; and Nebraska, 57.[3]

STATES' RIGHTS CAMPAIGN

Unfortunately, the Deep South led in the frequency of this loathsome offense. But most citizens of these states earnestly deplored lynchings and worked to eliminate completely these crimes against humanity. Some states' righters held that the states were effectively handling the problem and charged that if a federal anti-lynching law were enacted it would give the federal courts power to try a citizen in the courts of a state other than his own and hence deny him the right to a trial by a jury of his own peers. From the year 1965 to the time of this writing—a period of eight years—not one lynching has been officially recorded in the American nation according to records at Tuskegee Institute, the institution of higher learning established by Booker T. Washington.[4] That institution has for many years kept a record of lynchings committed. The concept of a federal government and separate sovereign states, each with separate and distinct powers, is a concept which should be preserved. But the powers granted to the federal government and to the separate states are accompanied by distinct responsibilities which must be upheld in order to preserve both the states and the federal government.

Early in 1948, backers of the idea of states' rights met to repudiate Truman's civil rights program. On February 8, southern governors manifested their concern and alarm. Meeting at Wakulla Springs, Florida, the governors named their own political action committee and appointed Governor Strom Thurmond of South Carolina to report to President Truman that the conference had decided that "the President's program, if enacted into law, would put the

South back in the dark days of Reconstruction." [5] Governor William Tuck asked the Virginia general assembly to bar the name of Truman from the 1948 ballot. Plans were made for a rump convention following the national Democratic convention in Philadelphia in early July.[6]

I recall that I was assigned the task to call a Southwide states rights preconvention caucus in Philadelphia on the Sunday afternoon just before the opening of the 1948 national Democratic convention. It was also decided to summon a small group of leaders in the movement to meet on Saturday afternoon at the Crystal Ballroom of the Benjamin Franklin Hotel, July 11, the day preceding the southern caucus. A telegram went to the following southern conservatives: Judge Tom Brady, Brookhaven, Mississippi; Arch Rowan, Fort Worth, Texas; Governor William Tuck, Richmond, Virginia; Leander Perez, Plaquemine, Louisiana; Judge Meredith Gibson, Longview, Texas; Governor Strom Thurmond, Columbia, South Carolina; John U. Barr, New Orleans, Louisiana; Bob Goodman, Birmingham, Alabama; Governor Ben Laney, Little Rock, Arkansas; J. M. Bonner, Camden, Alabama; George Warren, Hampton, South Carolina; Walter Sillers, Rosedale, Mississippi; E. H. Ramsey, Jacksonville, Florida; Leon Harris, Anderson, South Carolina; Jim Peterson, Manchester, Georgia; Frank Upchurch, St. Augustine, Florida; Governor Fielding Wright, Jackson, Mississippi; and Col. Marion Rushton, Birmingham, Alabama. From this list of names of southern conservative leaders it is obvious that the states'-rights effort was South-wide in effect. When the time for the advance meeting arrived practically all of the individuals who had received the telegram inviting them to the meeting were present.

As was to be expected, the groundwork for a convention fight had been laid. Several delegations from the South were challenged. Angry and concerned, the southern delegations assembled in Philadelphia prepared to offer the name of Governor Ben Laney of Arkansas as a candidate for the presidency.[7]

The Mississippi delegation, when questioned by the credentials committee, bluntly proclaimed "without apologies" its intention not to support President Truman in the November election.[8] The Mississippians were, nevertheless, able to obtain their seats in the convention. Although seating of the South Carolina delegation was challenged, the challenge was set aside by a vote of twenty-five to two.[9] The Democratic party manifested the desire to be as tolerant as possible with the recalcitrant southerners.

On the convention floor, however, an effort was made to punish the Mississippi delegation.[10] George Vaughn from Missouri, a black member of the credentials committee, amid catcalls and defiance, moved that the irreconcilable Mississippi delegation be unseated.[11] The convention, seeking unity, responded with a thunderous voice vote of "Noes."[12] A motion was made for a roll call vote, but the genial chairman, Senator Alben Barkley of Kentucky, declared the motion was defeated. This action did not satisfy some of the delegations seeking the ouster of Mississippi.

New York, California, and Illinois delegates managed to gain the floor and clearly stated they wanted it known that they favored unseating the Mississippi delegation.[13] Other states shouted their demand to be recorded as favoring the ouster. Included were Washington, Iowa, Minnesota, and the District of Columbia, making a total of 503 votes, or 115 short of a majority. During Vaughn's speech a Florida delegate shouted, "Shut him up." [14]

The southerners made a futile effort to restore the two-thirds rule for the nomination of candidates. This rule for many years had given the Solid South veto power over the rest of the convention. The convention responded with an overwhelming "No" to the restoration of this rule.[15]

Former governor Dan Moody of Texas proposed a states' rights plank sponsored by Texas, Alabama, Tennessee, Virginia, Mississippi, Georgia, Florida, and South Carolina.[16] The states' rights plank offered as a part of the Democratic party platform, set forth the following: "The Democratic Party reaffirms its adherence to the fundamental principle of states' rights as reserved in the Federal Constitution, and pledges that it will oppose any attempt, by legislation or otherwise, to invade the exclusive jurisdiction of the states in their domestic affairs."

The convention bluntly turned thumbs down on the proposed states' rights plank. Many indicated it would interfere with the civil rights program. This test of strength emphatically revealed that the southern position was disastrously weak. The vote was 925 to 309.[17]

Then came the battle of civil rights. By a roll call vote of 651½ to 582½ the convention demanded that four objectives of this program be spelled out: abolition of poll taxes in federal elections, a national law against lynching, creation of a permanent fair employment practices system, and non-segregation of the races in the armed services. Bilbo had discussed the same four-point program throughout the state of Mississippi and fought it within the United States Senate.[18]

Hubert Humphrey, mayor of Minneapolis, threw down the gauntlet in the convention. He demanded that the four-point civil rights program be spelled out without quibbling or equivocation. He insisted that it be written clearly and emphatically into the party platform. The Humphrey speech was followed by a demonstration which lasted nearly ten minutes. For the first time since the debate began, men and women bearing banners stepped into the aisles and started marching in the convention hall.

Shouted the mayor of Minneapolis, "We are 172 years late in acting. It is now time for the Democratic party to get out of the shadows of the states' rights and walk forthrightly in the bright sunshine of human rights and march down the high road of progressive democracy." [19]

Offered as an addition to the resolution of the platform committee's plank was the following: "We highly commend President Harry Truman on his courageous stand on the issue of civil rights. We call upon the Congress to support our president in guaranteeing these basic and fundamental rights."

Meanwhile the states' righters received a strategic setback. Senator John McClellan was prepared to present the name of Governor Ben Laney of Arkansas as a candidate for president, as had been earlier agreed, when Governor Laney suddenly announced he was withdrawing from the race.[20] The moment arrived when the Deep South states' rights delegates concluded, "This is the time." After months-long discussion and planning the moment for a walk-out had arrived.

Getting the floor was not easy. Finally, Hardy Ellis, chairman of the Alabama delegation, on the authority of "personal privilege," got the floor and stood before the microphone. "Mr. Chairman," he said, "My colleagues and I came here pledged to walk out of this convention if certain circumstances developed. We will proceed to do so." Then he shouted, "I am also authorized to announce that the Mississippi delegation is joining us." The convention was momentarily stunned as the Alabamians and Mississippians moved down one of the main aisles of the convention hall. Dr. John Minor Faser, for years dean of the school of pharmacy at the University of Mississippi, ran to the wall where the Mississippi banner was displayed, grabbed it, and held it high as he joined the exodus. Former governor Hugh White was in the lead, followed by twenty-two Mississippi delegates and one half of Alabama's delegation of twenty-six—all angry, defiant, and melodramatic.[21] I was one of the twenty-two Mississippi delegates who stalked out of that convention.

We marched down the aisle to the accompaniment of catcalls, threats, and some praise. One of the Missouri delegates said to the men passing him, "I wish we had the guts you fellows have." Several others remarked, "Good riddance to bad rubbish."

Weaver Gore, a Mississippi delegate, unbuttoned his shirt and said to me, "No one had better try to stop me.

I'll cut my way out of here." Across his chest was a belt to which was attached a scabbard containing a large Bowie knife. He expressed the feeling of the delegates who were on the march. A photograph taken of the delegates as they moved toward the door and later published in *Life* showed the delegates waving their arms in the air, their mouths opened wide as they shouted and held high the banners of their states. The spirit was "We're getting out of here. The hell with this convention."

Outside the convention hall, the delegates were confronted with a downpour of rain. A television official asked them to reenact the walkout for a national audience from a temporary studio set up in the convention building. A table was placed in front of the camera. The participating delegates formed a line and marched before the camera. Each threw his badge on the table while making an angry statement.[22] The rebel yells continued as the other delegates waited outside.

Howard Lanim, leader of the sixty-piece convention band, was twice approached by men who offered him a large sum of money to have the band play "Dixie" at a certain strategic moment of the convention. He remarked that the roll of money appeared to be five hundred dollars or more.[23] The "strategic" moment occurred when the delegates commenced their walk-out. The playing of "Dixie" would have aroused the old Civil War spirit and set the convention delegates from the South on fire. But when the delegates walked out, Lanim refused to accommodate the southerners and the band did not play.

Meanwhile, inside the convention hall, other southerners who questioned the wisdom of the walk-out seethed with anger. During this emotional situation, the convention hostess released forty-eight doves of peace, one representing each state.[24] The doves had been penned up for hours. In their eagerness for freedom the birds brushed against the heads of many prominent Democrats, "nearly knocking their heads off and thoroughly soiling a number of unfortunate spectators."

The remaining southerners nominated Senator Richard Russell of Georgia for president. The nine and one-half remaining southern delegations gave President Truman only thirteen votes.[25]

When President Truman received the nomination, he did a most unusual thing. Before a weary and fatigued convention of delegates, he delivered his acceptance speech at two o'clock in the morning.

Walter Sillers, respected legislator and Speaker of the House in Mississippi, announced, "With no postmortems, no recriminations, no regrets, on to Birmingham." [26] Governor Fielding Wright and the states' rights delegates left Philadelphia July 16 and headed for Birmingham accompanied by a large number of people from Alabama, Mississippi, Florida, Arkansas, Tennessee, Texas, Georgia, North Carolina, and South Carolina.[27] When the hotel convention hall in Birmingham proved to be too small to hold the crowd, the meeting was moved to a larger convention hall.

The decision was made to stage a full-fledged states' rights campaign to the end that neither Tom Dewey, the Republican; nor Henry Wallace, the independent; nor

Harry Truman, the Democrat, could achieve a majority. The lack of a majority would force the issue into the House of Representatives where each state would have but one vote. The idea was to place the states' righters in a strategic position and to compel the advocates of civil rights to withdraw their civil rights proposals or at least to achieve a compromise.[28] Observed Walter Sillers, "I believe we have an excellent chance to displace the voices of the New Deal Democrats so that the Jeffersonian faction will be recognized as the real national Democratic party." [29]

Many strong-willed men served at the helm of the states' rights campaign. Wally Wright, a wholesale merchant of Jackson and chairman of the states' rights organization, reminded me of General "Blood and Guts" Patton. He called many meetings. His policy was to have all resolutions prepared in advance. The morning meetings were devoted to individuals seeking to get things off their chests. Anyone who had something to say was permitted to say it. The afternoon meetings were given to the adoption of the prepared resolutions. George Godwin, an advertising executive, was the idea man behind the movement. Judge Merritt Gibson of Longview, Texas, was the campaign chairman. Frank Dixon, a former Alabama governor, was a strong leader in the effort.

The leadership of the anti-civil rights effort did not like the terminology *Dixiecrat* because they were trying to make this a national movement. The term *Dixiecrat* suggested a provincial approach.

The states' righters unanimously nominated Governor

Strom Thurmond of South Carolina for president and Governor Fielding Wright of Mississippi for vice-president. Both were dedicated and sincere men and firmly believed that the civil rights program was a threat to America. I traveled on alternate weeks with these two candidates.

Two incidents stand out in my memory of these two stalwarts. Governor Wright, a timid man, was driving the car in which we were riding across a bridge connecting Mississippi and Louisiana. He saw a Louisiana highway patrol delegation waiting to escort him to Tallulah and cautioned me, "Look straight ahead and maybe they won't recognize us." When the waiting patrolmen did not recognize the governor, he remarked, "That was a close call but we made it."

Strom Thurmond, now a national figure and a thorough gentleman, could move a crowd to applause whenever he wished. When he stood on his toes, raised his arms above his head, and increased the tempo of his voice, the crowd invariably broke out with enthusiastic applause.

Patriotism was a factor in the states rights campaign. For example, Governor Strom Thurmond, speaking as a candidate for the presidency during the campaign said at Lexington, Virginia. "I am not a stranger in Virginia. In Virginia I feel at home for here I am among my own people. My forebear, John Thurmond, came from Virginia. My grandfather on my father's side was named after a great Virginian. His name was George Washington Thurmond and he was with General Robert E. Lee, another great Virginian, when Lee surrendered at Appomattox. Like Lee and Washington, Thurmond, was a patriot. He

STATES' RIGHTS CAMPAIGN

fought in three wars, the Mexican war, the Indian wars, and with the Confederacy in that terrible crisis of 1860 to 1865. After my grandfather left General Lee he walked all the way from Appomattox to Edgefield, South Carolina."

I well remember accompanying Governor Sam Jones of Louisiana to a press conference in Minnesota and to a states' rights meeting in Bismarck, North Dakota. The campaign had generated relatively little interest in that part of the country. One strange fact of the campaign was that the states' rights representative in North Dakota bore the name Jim Crow.

The one mistake in judgment made by the states' righters was that they underestimated Harry Truman. Columnists Joseph and Stewart Alsop wrote of him. "A new Truman was on view. The Missourian had decided to campaign like a county sheriff in the Ozarks." [30] He said he would be elected without the South—and he was.

The effects of the states' rights campaign are difficult to calculate. The movement carried Louisiana, Mississippi, Alabama, and South Carolina and captured thirty-nine electoral votes. As the civilian counterpart of the War Between the States it kept alive for a few years longer the "traditions" of a dead century. Despite the dedication and vigor of its proponents, it represented another instance of negative thinking and a further indication of the failure to recognize reality. The campaign's most effective result was that it solidified the spirit which in the years to follow was expressed in the words "Never, never, never."

These words became the campaign call for the repeated

failures of negativism. These words created a false hope for the negative extremists and delayed a program of positive political action which held the potential for advancing the best interests of all the people of the South, white and black. The cry, "Never, never, never," was uttered with a pseudo sense of patriotism in the spirit of the earlier cry in history, "Remember the Alamo." But the cry of the Alamo was the patriotic call of freedom. "Never, never, never," was the demand for the continuity of slavery. Men were blinded by a conflict of heritages. "Remember the Alamo" was tied to the sacred concepts of constitutional freedom; "Never, never, never," was tied to nullification, interposition, closing down of schools, and other forms of inevitable failure.

In the final days of 1972 Harry Truman joined that great caravan moving out into eternity. Wilson Minor of the New Orleans *Times-Picayune* contacted Walter Dent May, last surviving member of the nine states rights electors from Mississippi who cast their votes against the Democratic presidential nominee, and asked if he had had a personal change of heart concerning the former president?

"Yes, I was wrong about him," replied Mr. May who as a young attorney in 1948 voted against Harry Truman. "In retrospect," he said, "Harry Truman was more of a steadying influence on our country than we realized then."

NOTES TO CHAPTER 8

[1] New York *Times*, July 15, 1948, p. 7.
[2] Daniel T. Williams, *Compiled Record of Tuskegee Institute* (Tuskegee, Ala. "Lynching Records," 1969), 9.

STATES' RIGHTS CAMPAIGN

[3] *Ibid.*, 6. [4] *Ibid.*, 10.
[5] McComb (Miss.) *Enterprise-Journal*, August 3, 1948.
[6] New York *Times*, July 15, 1948, p. 8. [7] *Ibid.*
[8] *Ibid.*, July 14, 1948, p. 5. [9] *Ibid.*
[10] New York *Times*, July 14, 1948, p. 6. [11] *Ibid.* [12] *Ibid.*
[13] *Ibid.* [14] *Ibid.* [15] *Ibid.* [16] *Ibid.*, July 15, 1948, p. 8.
[17] McComb (Miss.) *Enterprise-Journal*, July 16, 1948.
[18] New York *Times*, July 15, 1948, p. 8. [19] *Ibid.* [20] *Ibid.*
[21] "Candidate Truman Comes Out Fighting," *Life*, XXV (July 26, 1948), 15-20.
[22] Jackson (Miss.) *Daily News*, July 16, 1948.
[23] New York *Times*, July 15, 1948, p. 8.
[24] "Candidate Truman," 15.
[25] New York *Times*, July 15, 1948, p. 8.
[26] McComb (Miss.) *Enterprise-Journal*, July 16, 1948, p. 1.
[27] *Ibid.*, July 17, 1948, p. 1. [28] *Ibid.*
[29] *Ibid.*, July 19, 1948, p. 1. [30] "Candidate Truman," 15.

9 Outside the Mainstream of America

PRIOR TO THE U.S. Supreme Court's historic school decision of May 17, 1950, a black mother called at my newspaper office. Addressing me by name, she said, "Mr. Emmerich, I'm in deep trouble and I need your help." I asked her to tell me about her problem.

She replied, "My son is in the county jail. They have charged him with breaking into a business house. My boy said he didn't do it and because he insists that he didn't do it they beat him." Then, with a show of emotion, she pled, "I want a doctor to help him. He's in pain."

I contacted a law enforcement officer whom I thought would cooperate with me. He admitted, "That black was whipped, but I didn't have anything to do with it." Then, to my surprise, he volunteered to slip the eighteen-year-old out of the jail and bring him to my office. I arranged with the late Dr. S. Paul Klotz, a beloved local family physician, to be at the office when the prisoner arrived. The young black lowered his britches so the physician could examine his badly lacerated and bruised buttocks. After Dr. Klotz had treated him with ointment and other medicine, the boy was returned to jail.

Although I knew the story would be unpopular, the newspaper carried an account of the incident. The readers' general reaction to the story proved that my apprehensions were not without foundation. During that era, anyone who failed to conform to the rigid philosophy of the time aroused devastating accusations of treachery to the white race. I soon realized that my exposé of the jailhouse whipping would probably cause repercussions.

A Democratic primary, then tantamount to an election, was held that week. In that day, many newspapers staged so-called "election parties," and the newspaper office was headquarters for gathering and unofficially tabulating the election results. During an election party, the street in front of the newspaper office was blocked off and massive bulletin boards containing the names of all of the candidates were erected. It was an expensive and arduous task. Large crowds turned out, and most of the people remained until three or four o'clock in the morning to see how their favorite candidates had fared.

The office that hot night was crowded with people. I left the microphone of the loudspeaker system to get some fresh air. As I moved among the crowd one man, his voice quivering slightly, confronted me with this question: "Why did you print that story about that nigger being whipped in the jail?"

I replied, "Because it was a legitimate story and I could not have done otherwise without being irresponsible." After a series of questions, each more belligerent than the previous one, I finally stated, "If we do not stop these abuses ourselves the time will come when others will force us to correct them." As I turned to walk away, I felt a hard fist strike the back of my neck, just behind my right ear. I plummeted to the ground—out cold. I don't know how one measures the time he is out, but somehow I felt I had been knocked out to the count of four, possibly five, when friends lifted me to my feet and led me back into my office. I was still groggy for several moments. The following day I learned that a fund was being raised to hire a lawyer to defend my assailant.

An interesting aspect of the story is that a month later, the black youth who had been beaten in jail was released after another man confessed to the crime.

I would not be fair if I did not add that the man who struck me later was contrite and apologized earnestly. His apology was voluntary, genuine, and sincere. I would say that today he wants all men, black and white, to be treated fairly. Despite our unfortunate initial encounter, we became friends; and since then he has repeatedly proved his friendship for me. This incident is but one illustration of the change in attitude which has occurred in the Deep South.

The Deep South was in many ways outside the mainstream of American life. An effort made by the Mississippi chapter of Sigma Delta Chi, professional journalism fraternity, to host its national convention reflects the attitude held by many persons outside Mississippi. In 1958 the Mississippi chapter of the society was strong and ambitious. Wilson Minor, Mississippi correspondent for the New Orleans *Times-Picayune*, was president when the chapter decided to invite the national organization to hold its 1960 annual convention in Jackson. A committee of four was named to attend the 1958 annual convention in Indianapolis, Indiana, and extend the invitation. This committee consisted of: Minor; Dick Sanders, news director of television station WLBT of Jackson; Phil Stroupe, a staff member of the Jackson *State Times;* and I, who at the time was editor of the *State Times.*

Notwithstanding the fact that committees from two major cities were also seeking the convention, the Sigma Delta Chi directors gave the green light to Jackson. Shortly thereafter, however, the Chicago chapter of Sigma Delta Chi announced its opposition to holding a convention in Jackson. Other chapters expressed similar reluctance.

"What about black delegates?" they asked. At that time the problem of public accommodations for blacks was admittedly a matter of conflict within the state. The Mississippi committee announced that any black delegates to the convention would be housed at Jackson State College and cars would be placed at their disposal. In spite of the fact that only two black delegates had attended the 1957 convention, the proposed convention site encountered opposition.

Some members of the national board of directors of Sigma Delta Chi suggested privately to the Mississippi delegates that it would be wise for them to withdraw the invitation. We complied. Plans to hold the convention of six hundred or more editors and journalistic students in Jackson was cancelled. The Deep South was, indeed, still outside the mainstream of American life, a fact which constituted a basic reason for migration from the region, particularly among young people who moved away and contributed their talents toward the betterment of states in other regions of the country.

10 Soul Searching

I WILLINGLY CONFESS that I, too, have been victimized by the philosophy of backwardness which for more than a hundred years plagued the Deep South. Despite the fact that I have cringed at the thoughts of slavery and servitude, have long held that no American citizen should be disfranchised, and have tried to pursue the cause of racial justice.

Shortly after the United States Supreme Court outlawed the "separate-but-equal" school concept, I was invited by national leaders of the Methodist church to present the southern viewpoint on a four-man panel meeting in Chicago. Roy Wilkins, executive secretary of the NAACP, was one of the other three panelists. Asked to present an "academic" viewpoint, I found myself hammering on such subjects as illegitimacy, venereal diseases, crime, and the like. I told Mr. Wilkins his people had to recognize the black man's responsibility for these problems. Obviously, I was overlooking the cause of these things—the long years of slavery.

Methodist leaders also asked me to present the southern viewpoint before an audience in the coliseum on the campus of Southern Methodist University in Dallas. One of the other three panelists was Thurgood Marshall. What was this southern viewpoint I was asked to present? By no means was it toleration of injustice, arson, and bombing. Yet I found myself before a liberal-minded audience clashing with Thurgood Marshall, now Justice Marshall, of the United States Supreme Court. Some of my remarks brought forth a few scattered boos. When I returned home, however, many persons who had seen and heard the program on television or had read about it in the newspapers were enthusiastic over my comments. This reaction, I admit, perplexed me somewhat, and I pondered the reason.

Adding to the pressure of the cottonfield philosophy was the historical reminder that the black people first enslaved their own and in turn sold them to white slave traders. God fortified Nigeria. Her streams leading from the hinterland have dangerous rapids. The seashores are shallow. Years ago black people captured their brothers and delivered them to ships anchored at a safe distance offshore.

But how we think is influenced by where we live. If a boy from Mississippi moved to Vermont, the odds are that as a man he would think as a Vermonter. And if a boy from Vermont were reared in Mississippi, the odds are that as a man he would think as a Mississippian.

In 1955 Carl Rowan, a black reporter for the Minneapolis *Star-Tribune*, visited in my office. Since that time Rowan has served as United States ambassador to Finland and as director of the United States Information Agency, a post held by the late, popular, Edward R. Murrow. Today Rowan writes a syndicated newspaper column.

In 1971 Rowan again visited McComb. In an article in the August, 1971, issue of *Ebony*, a nationally circulated black-oriented magazine, he pointed to the changes which had occurred in the South between his visits of 1955 and 1971.[1]* He used two communities as examples of these epochal changes—the home of his youth, McMinnville, Tennessee, and McComb, Mississippi. Referring to our meeting in 1955 he said, "As I pressed the troubled Emmerich, he rationalized with talk about Negro illegitimacy and crimes in Mississippi, about the educational and cultural lag of the blacks." Then he added, "Emmerich said, "It's not our fault if the Negro is only a century away from the jungle. I say that's just not enough time to civilize people.' " Rowan continued, "I answered Emmerich in my third book *Go South to Sorrow* when I asked, 'How many centuries does it take to lift men out of the jungle and teach them to tie a cotton gin fan to a fourteen-year-old boy's multilated body and dump it into a river?' " [2]

I must say that Rowan did not continue in this militant vein as he wrote about the significant changes that had taken place in McComb during the sixteen years between 1955 and 1971, changes which he acknowledged that I, along with many other persons, had helped to bring about. If southerners are willing to do a little personal soul-searching and weigh the attitudes of 1955 and 1971 we can sense the effects of what I call the "cottonfield philosophy"—and my reason for saying that I was victimized by it. It was a form of thought control.

I listened to a lecture by Dr. John Furbay, an international representative of Trans-World Airlines.[3] He has worked closely with people fresh out of the tribal bush

* Notes appear at end of chapter.

country of Africa. He reports meeting persons who had never seen a wheel as well as first-generation people from this background who had learned to operate complicated machines.[4] He remarked, "An African, with the same education, can learn as fast as any other race of people." He used the Ethiopian Air Lines as an example and reported that men just one generation removed from the tribal bush regions are piloting and maintaining the largest jet planes. The Ethiopian Air Lines has one of the best safety records among the air lines of the world. He said that the safety record attained by the airline points up "millions of right decisions" made by the African natives.[5]

Before the Wright brothers flew a plane at Kitty Hawk, they investigated an invention of the Australian aborigines, who had put into use the laws which enable a plane to be lifted into the air.[6] Because of the special profile of the arms of the Australian boomerang, the air exerts a force on them which is directed from the flatter, lower side to the more convex or upper side. The same force is exerted on the wings of an airplane.

The space age dates from the day an Australian aborigine first whittled the crotch of an acacia tree into a flat, sickle-shaped blade for use as a hunting weapon. The fact that people so close to the Stone Age can be mentioned in the same breath with aerodynamics challenges everyone to re-examine old ideas and age-old cliches.[7]

Throughout the years the "cottonfield philosophy" was in evidence in my own community, a community close to my heart. During the thirties, I published photographs of the white schools in the county, one each issue until the series was completed. In general the schools were modern, comfortable, attractive buildings. The citizens were highly responsive to this feature, and a number of parents called me to say "Thank you."

Then, as planned, I also published photographs of the Negro schools. They revealed slums—dilapidated shacks, old barn-like structures, deteriorating churches, and such unpainted structures as are referred to as a "lean-to." The response to this series of photographs was generally resentful. Many readers expressed their displeasure.

The Burglundtown school, the Negro school in a black section of town, was a frame building situated in a low-lying area. When it rained the school yard was flooded. Children had to wade knee-deep in water to get to the muddy road in front of the school. The late X. A. Kramer, mayor of the city, was a resourceful individual. He said, "Let's capitalize on this flood situation." The school children, the teachers, and a photographer agreed to cooperate when the next big rain occurred. As the children waded to the road, most of them knee-deep in water, the photographer took graphic pictures. Kramer took the pictures to Washington, made an appeal to some political leaders, and came home with the promise of a grant to help build a new school for the black children.

Once I heard two men talking. One said, "Where did you get the money to buy those new basketball uniforms for the team?" The other, a school trustee, replied, "We found a little extra money in the 'nigger' school fund and used it." The idea of a school system founded on the then constitutional "separate but equal" plan was a myth.

In those early years civic leaders in McComb worked closely with the Veterans Administration in an effort to have a veterans hospital located in the city. The leaders became highly enthusiastic over the project and virtually every business man in town sent a telegram to both the political leaders in Washington and to the officials of the V.A. Popular administrators of two veterans hospitals were cooperating with the local committees. The number of V.A. representatives who visited the city and the statements made in a V.A. house organ as well as comments made by V.A. officials led members of the community to believe that the hospital would be achieved. Announced as a twelve-million-dollar investment, the hospital would have been a valuable addition to the community and its economy. When a report was circulated that the hospital was to be for Negro patients the attitude of the community switched. Businessmen were asked to remove their names from previously signed petitions. The rule of conformity was immediately applied. Telegrams were sent to the Veterans Administration expressing opposition. An opposition committee went to Washington to see the director of the Veterans Administration. Petitions opposing the building of the hospital were circulated. I witnessed one man present the petition to a fellow citizen with the question, "Do you want some black son-of-a-bitch from Detroit to move into town and push your wife off the sidewalk?" The second citizen replied, "No." Then said the first man, "Well, sign here." And the second man signed the petition.

The original petitioning committee returned to Washington and contacted General Omar Bradley, war hero and at that time director of the Veterans Administration. Bradley stated, "We can't afford risking having the hospital dynamited." The committee asked, "Why do you think the hospital would be dynamited?" The general responded, "The opposition committee that came up here a couple of days ago told me that if the hospital was built that there are people down there who would dynamite it."

During the fifties many black people were unemployed. Although McComb Manufacturing Company, a garment plant, needed labor in order to expand, the rule of the day was that blacks could not be employed in regional garment plants.

A plan whereby a branch plant could be established in an available building in a black area was discussed with Dick Busby, manager of the McComb Manufacturing Company. Such an arrangement could provide woefully needed jobs for Negro women. The first step was to have some sewing machines located in the black school and teachers available to train these people. The machines were installed. The idea had not been discussed generally until someone began to spread information about the plan and the effort became town talk. Someone then charged that the white schools were being discriminated against and said machines should be placed in the white schools also. The proposition finally reached the board of directors of a prestigious organization in town, and the plan to develop jobs for the black jobless while providing a new labor source for plant expansion, was defeated.

In 1962 the Deep South, particularly the state of Mississippi, was lambasted in headlines throughout the world because of extremist activities. I contacted *Life* magazine and said all aspects of race relations in the Deep South were not negative, that there were some positive aspects of the problem, and that some whites and Negroes were friends.

Life sent two of its top staffers, a photographer and a writer, to McComb. I worked very closely with them during the month they spent in town. In the issue of May 7, 1962, *Life* published nine full pages on the story of race relations in McComb.[8] It was a fair story, did not gloss over the ugly side, but did give instances of both the conflicts and the harmony of the racial story. Nevertheless, few people in the United States were privileged to read it since it was published in *Life International*, a magazine with a format similar to the domestic issue, which goes to seventy-odd nations around the world. The copies I eventually received were sent from Paris after a long delay.

During the 1962 convention of the Pan American Press Association in New Orleans it was my privilege to attend a dinner given for a group of sixteen editors. Seated across the table from me was the editor of *Life International*. I asked him if the story would be published in the domestic issue of *Life*. He replied that he had every reason to think that it would be. Others close to *Life* expressed the same opinion.

In no way did I take offense at *Life*'s use of the story—"Dilemma in Mississippi." After all, it was *Life*'s story and

Life's decision; but I could not refrain from wondering why the narration with the two sides of the country's big news story of that day was shipped abroad.

I began to look objectively at newspaper journalism to determine whether it was exercising racial justice in reporting. The general practice, not particularly planned or even consciously conceived, was to publish photographs of Negroes who committed brutal crimes. Yet very rarely was a black's photograph published when he distinguished himself or in anyway achieved something constructive. Some newspapers ran news about black people under the condescending caption, "With Our Colored Friends."

A metropolitan black-oriented newspaper, carried a news report in which I was involved. At that time, white-oriented newspapers consistently designated race when black people were mentioned in print. A story would indicate, "Joe Doe, black," or "John Doe, Negro" to be certain that the Negro of the story was tied securely to his race. I well remember my reaction when the black newspaper, conversely pursuing the same pattern, printed the following lead line: "J. O. Emmerich, white."

Recognizing that responsible journalism demanded reform, we decided to use more copy involving black people. Our initial plan was to segregate the news, printing one edition for white subscribers and another for blacks. The reasoning behind this scheme was the fact that many white readers resented news involving black people and considered the presence of such news an intrusion. Although the blacks were exerting no pressure for the newspaper to print more copy regarding their activities, it was a matter of conscience and the knowledge that the community would be improved by upgrading the black people just as conversely it was damaged by degrading them. The plan of segregated editions, however, did not succeed. No practical way could be devised to segregate deliveries of the newspaper, and problems arose when black editions reached the homes of white readers.

The first major reform in news policy was to use titles in referring to black people. When the first issue referring to married black women as *Mrs.* and to single black women as *Miss* hit the streets, the reactions were immediate. A few white people were horrified by the thought.

An elderly man obviously angry came to the newspaper office and complained, "Our niggers are already uppity enough. Are you trying to make them more uppity?" I told him that a title costs nothing; that the term *Mrs.* indicates only that a woman is married. On the other hand, I said, the failure to use titles is basically a denial of human dignity. According black persons simple human dignity is a means of giving them a sense of well being. I tried to explain that titles require neither government appropriations nor the expenditure of private money. On the contrary, I said, the recognition of human dignity is nothing short of common courtesy.

Finally, the newspaper staff concluded that news is news, and no journalistic principle requires that news be measured against its involvement with race. This policy meant there would be no limitations on the publication of news insofar as race was concerned. This policy was by no means applied overnight. The sensitivities of our readers were carefully considered; after all, the new policy, which none could deny was just and responsible, had to compete in spirit with a contrary news policy which had reigned supreme for more than a century. Reporting black weddings and similar news created delicate moments for the newspaper. But in the end, the success of a policy which upheld the basic American concept of human dignity provided additional evidence of the changes which were coming to pass in the Deep South.

NOTES TO CHAPTER 10

[1] Carl Rowan, "South of Freedom, 1971," *Ebony*, XXIV (August, 1971), 134.
[2] *Ibid.*
[3] John Furbay, "Countdown for Tomorrow," Lecture No. XCTV87688, recorded by Columbia Records.
[4] *Ibid.*   [5] *Ibid.*
[6] Felix Hess, "The Aerodynamics of Boomerangs," *Scientific American*, CCXIX (November, 1968), 128.
[7] Dale Rudolph, "Boomerang: The Stick That Returns," *Popular Mechanics*, CXXI (April, 1964), 156-58.
[8] "Dilemma in Mississippi," *Life International*, XXII (May 7, 1962), 15-23.

11 "Go to Jail First"

THE TWO FACES of Janus, one looking in, the other looking out, is a symbol of the South. For the South has not one, but two separate and distinct heritages. First is the American heritage of liberty, with the constitutional concepts of freedom for all people and respect for the dignity of the individual. The second heritage—the southern heritage—has its roots in slavery. The incompatibility of the two has been a source of frustration to southern people and is at the base of the emotional reactions often experienced when the conflicts of the two heritages have been brought under close scrutiny.

If we are honest with ourselves, we will agree that these two heritages are a fact in the history of the South. We are both southerners and Americans, but during some periods in recent decades we have been confronted by problems which often made it difficult for us to be true southerners and true Americans at the same time.

This conflict in heritages often has made it difficult for statesmanship to prevail in the Deep South. Statesmanship consists in recognizing a challenge and coping with it before it degenerates into a crisis. The conflict between our two heritages has been a source of emotional struggle. It is difficult for statesmanship to prevail when people are not objective, and yet people find it hard to be objective when they are emotional.

When people are objective, they can recognize impending challenges. When they are emotional, however, they cannot always recognize truth. Not to be forgotten is the unquestioned fact that challenges are inevitable. They come with time and change. Thus one face of Janus looks inward at the emotions of the people, while the other peers outward hopefully, perhaps, in the direction of objectivity.

Too often when leaders with objectivity have sought to warn against impending problems they have been shouted down. It is always easier to arouse the suspicions of the masses—to anger, frighten, or frustrate them—than to make them think.

In the years following 1954, the attitude of the South was about the same as that of 1860. Although there was talk of secession, the majority of southern people could comprehend the folly of such a move. There was talk of closing down schools, an action which would have been tantamount to an even greater form of secession—secession from civilization.

The challenge today is to develop the willingness to face realities. In short, we must overcome the historically nurtured philosophy of backwardness. Today, a century after the mass blood-letting, many Deep South residents continue to believe that the war was a glorifying event. It was, however, a tragic blunder, a needless mistake, an historic error. The mistake is compounded if we continue to permit history to repeat itself through our unwillingness to face reality while striving to perpetuate the status quo.

In 1961 Louisiana held first place among the states in illiteracy. South Carolina ranked second, and Mississippi was in third place.[1]* Mississippi's per capita income that year was $1,229, against a national average of $2,263. The median annual income for white families was $4,209; for black families it was $1,444.[2] Obviously, both poverty and educational status were factors in what was then about to happen in Mississippi.

James Meredith, the twenty-nine-year-old Air Force veteran, applied for admittance to the University of Mississippi.[3] He was refused and appealed to the courts. Federal district judge Sidney C. Mize dismissed the case on the grounds that no racial discrimination had been proved.

Governor Ross Barnett told the people that the University of Mississippi would not be integrated while he was governor of the state of Mississippi. Residents throughout the state found comfort in his promise and believed he had some secret legal ace up his sleeve.

Tempers were soon at the boiling point in all of the Deep South states. Atrocities were being committed across the Southland, but Deep South crimes were most pronounced. Ross Barnett, chief executive of the state of Mississippi, stepped to the forefront as this crisis mounted. In June, 1962, the United States Court of Appeals for the Fifth Circuit reversed Judge Mize's decision and stated

* Notes appear at end of chapter.

that Meredith had been rejected "solely because he was a Negro" and ordered his admission to Ole Miss.

Then followed months of legal wrangling. Judge Ben F. Cameron, described by Claude Sitton in the New York *Times* as "a dedicated segregationist," said that the Fourteenth Amendment should not be enforced in the South. The panel of judges that had decided the case vacated the stay, but Judge Cameron issued three more in succession.[4] The case was placed before Justice Hugo L. Black of the U. S. Supreme Court, acting as circuit justice for the fifth circuit. He ordered the judgment of the circuit panel into effect at once. The time for a legal showdown had arrived.[5]

On September 13, 1962, following the discredited path of Governor Orval Faubus of Arkansas and Governor Jimmie Davis of Louisiana, Governor Ross Barnett took the case to the people. That eventful night he announced on state-wide television: "Even as I speak to you tonight the enemy is pouring across our borders. Already we hear the clash of resounding arms."[6] The state became the Virginia Assembly, and the ghost of Patrick Henry slipped into the homes of the people.

"I speak to you in the moment of our greatest crisis since the War Between the States," the governor drawled defiantly. "In the absence of Constitutional authority, and without legal action, an ambitious federal government, employing naked and arbitrary power, has decided to deny us the right of self-determination in the conduct of our sovereign state." Continuing his blast he charged further, "Having long since failed in his efforts to conquer, the

"GO TO JAIL FIRST"

enemy is trying to break the indomitable spirit of our people and their unshakable will to preserve the sovereign majesty of our Commonwealth, now seeks to break us physically with the power of force." [7]

This "enemy" the governor was verbally attacking was the United States of America and the stars and stripes to which all good Americans pledge allegiance, "one nation, under God, indivisible, with liberty and justice for all."

It was at this point in the challenge of the sixties that the defiant term "Never, never, never" became a rally cry for those resisting the black Americans' fight for equal rights. Exhorted Governor Barnett, "We must submit to unlawful dictates of the federal government or stand up like men and tell them 'Never.' We must not submit to moral degradation, to the shame and ruin that has been forced upon all others who lacked the courage to defend their beliefs."

In his call for war in this Deep South drama, Governor Barnett tied his appeal to the emotion-packed moments of American history. "Generations ago," he proclaimed, "our ancestors pledged their fortunes and their sacred honor to establish on this continent a government of the people, by the people, and for the people.[8] Succeeding generations defended their liberties with blood, sweat, and tears at Valley Forge, at Shiloh, and Vicksburg, in the Argonne, at Guadalcanal, and on the Heartbreak Hills of Korea. Our generation now faces a challenge to our liberties. The burning question in the minds of all Americans today is whether, in this crisis, we shall exhibit the same courage, devotion, and deathless principles, and the same determination to guarantee the blessings of liberty to future generations as was shown by those who had gone before." Governor Barnett's speech included unquoted quotes from Patrick Henry's "Give me liberty or give me death" speech, from Abraham Lincoln's Gettysburg Address, from the Declaration of Independence, from the preamble to the United States Constitution, and from the "Blood, sweat and tears" appeal of General Giuseppe Garibaldi to his troops in Italy which Winston Churchill made even more famous in his victory speech of World War II.

"We shall not drink from this cup of genocide," exclaimed the governor.[9]

Aroused was the fear of invasion, the thought of death and tyranny. And out of the frustrations that followed came the incentive to bomb, to burn, to dynamite.

One senator, orating on the floor of the state senate, said with a flare of emotion, "Every effort must be expended to win this battle regardless of the cost in lives."

Said another excitedly, "No man in a lifetime ever had the opportunity to witness the courage and the determination of such a governor."

In 1962 a new generation witnessed a rehearsal of the tragic fervor and costly emotionalism of 1860 which led to the needless mass blood-letting, burning, and bankruptcy of the Southland.

With the lone exception of Frank Smith, a lame duck representative who had been gerrymandered out of his post by the legislative reapportionment and the census of 1960, all Mississippi congressmen wired Governor Barnett expressing approval of his profound and belligerent speech.

State officials gave immediate press releases upholding the governor's militant stand. The House of Representatives, by a vote of 130 to 2, adopted a resolution supporting the governor's virtual declaration of war against the United States of America.[10] In the corridor of a federal court building a song rang out, "God help us to keep calm, cool, and segregated." State and local officials on all sides congratulated Barnett on his stand.

Friends spoke of Governor Barnett as "Good Ol' Ross." Some just referred to him as "Ol' Ross." He had more personal refinement than Bilbo but was not so sagacious or adroit. He possessed a homespun warmth that drew people to him.

So volatile was the moment that Mississippi needed a battle cry, one with the stimulating force of "Remember the Alamo," "Remember the Maine," "Remember Pearl Harbor," or, as the British would say, "Remember the Black Hole of Calcutta." Governor Barnett provided the phrase when he challenged all officials to "Go to Jail First," meaning to pledge themselves to ignore any official orders served upon them by the courts and allow themselves to be incarcerated rather than submit to federal authority. So the jailhouse became the symbol of patriotism, like the Liberty Bell, Independence Hall, and the written copy of the Declaration of Independence.

So seriously dedicated were the people to this symbol of freedom that anyone who became articulate in the name of restraint was regarded as a traitor and was condemned. "Go to Jail First" became the shouted words wherever crowds gathered. People recalled the day when Governor

Theodore G. Bilbo was jailed for contempt of court and from his cell announced as a candidate for governor—a position to which he was elected.

One night in 1962, forty thousand fans had assembled in the Memorial Stadium in Jackson for the annual gridiron contest between the University of Kentucky and the University of Mississippi. Governor Ross Barnett stepped from a car and walked toward his box seat near the sideline where the Ole Miss team would sit. A roar from the fans acknowledged the governor's entrance, and they stood up shouting, "Speech, speech."

Ol' Ross made his way to a microphone. He smiled jovially, his characteristic smile. He hesitated a few seconds and then proclaimed, "I love Mississippi." The fans roared. He continued, "I love the people of Mississippi." The crowd cheered again. Then said Ross, "I love the traditions of Mississippi." He sat down and the crowd stood up. Ross waved back to them, enjoying the moment of a conquering hero. The following day was a day of infamy—the day of chemicals and stones tossed at federal marshals, talk of throwing up breastworks preparatory to the battle—and deaths on the campus of the University of Mississippi. The events were chronicled around the world and written into the history books to be read by future generations.

During this period of alarm and excitement, a rumor was circulated that federal marshals "were on their way to get Ross." One Jacksonian, his eyes blazing with excitement, ran down the street, knocking on doors and warning the people, "We have got to protect our homes and our governor." A crowd gathered at the governor's

"GO TO JAIL FIRST"

mansion and circled it with manpower to resist any possible effort which might be made to "arrest Ross."

Editorially, I had expressed the opinion that it was a time to act with caution, that interfering with the legal processes of the university could result in its disaccreditation which would be disastrous to the cause of higher education in the state.

Editorially, I had expressed the opinion—far too mildly—that if Governor Barnett succeeded in his rash approach to the problem it would be the first time in the history of the United States that a United States Supreme Court decision had been set aside by a governor. Also I hoped Governor Barnett was as wise as he was courageous.[11] I commented further that the governor was severely damaging the image of the state and ignoring the processes of constitutional government.

As a result, an organized circulation boycott was directed against our newspaper. This reaction was understandable considering the oneness of the loyalty to the governor's expressed determination not to permit a decision of the United States Supreme Court to apply to his state.

People calling to cancel their subscriptions, used identical language: "I want to cancel my subscription to the *Enterprise-Journal*, and I want you to know that it is part of an organized campaign." A few were profane and enlarged upon the conversation, but by far the majority of callers were polite.

Committees called upon advertisers and requested that they discontinue advertising in the newspaper. The committee had little effect, however, because advertisers buy space to sell merchandise. The boycott on circulation was between 4 to 5 percent effective. All cancellations were carefully filed; and within a couple of months, after the fever of stimulated emotionalism had died down, circulation was back to normal. Six months later the newspaper showed a circulation gain.

About a year earlier, the newspaper had become involved in its efforts to discourage violence. During 1961, many "freedom riders" came to this community. There were harrassment arrests and some violence. The newspaper discouraged violence, pled for law and order, and urged that an effort be made not to project an ugly image of the state. The freedom riders were generally resented by the local citizens who presented dozens of arguments as to why the outsiders should "mind their own business" and "reform their own home communities." As a result of this resentment, five out-of-state newspapermen were beaten up just outside the newspaper office.

The following Sunday morning a stranger walked up to me. He seemed agreeable enough. I learned later he was a former Texas oil field worker. He stopped me and asked pleasantly, "Are you the fellow who runs this newspaper here?"

I answered affirmatively. Without warning, his fist smashed into my eyeglasses. I had just been released from the city hospital a couple of weeks before following a serious heart attack. My assailant later came to trial and was acquitted.

Contrary to what many people believed, a majority of the Deep South residents were not racists.[12] The population

"GO TO JAIL FIRST"

was divided between racists and conformists. Included among the racists were the extremists. It is the historic pattern. And not to be forgotten is the fact that conformity is a part of the philosophy of backwardness.

The problems confronted were historic ones, created years ago. No living person could be accused of creating them. What history put into the minds of people made the problem inevitable.

During these years the people of the region talked primarily about one subject—race. Let a group get together and it was a safe bet that this subject would come up and take over.

Although I knew that I was not on the friendliest basis with many people of my state, I did try to think objectively, to search for the truth. Objective thinking consistently brought me back to the same position. First, that the Deep South inevitably would be compelled to recognize the challenges involved; and second, that a nation with constitutional government could not survive if its constitution were not upheld.

At a cocktail party my wife and I attended, everyone was discussing the race issue. A dozen conversations were going on simultaneously, all about the black intrusion. On a note pad I sketched a likeness of two palm trees on an isolated island in the sea, with the waves lapping against the shore. I folded it, handed it to a friend, and asked that he pass it along to my wife. She unfolded the slip of paper, turned to me, and smiled. Several weeks later I observed that my wife had put my drawing of the two palm trees on a lonely island in the family Bible. I knew at least that she understood.

There must be a postscript to this chapter. When Governor Ross Barnett said to the 40,000 emotionally-moved gridiron fans, "I love the traditions of Mississippi" he was the conquering hero, perhaps as popular as Jefferson Davis at the time he was elected president of the Confederacy. On the other hand, when Governor Barnett later ran for another term of office, he finished fourth in a race of seven, garnering 75,741 votes of the total 603,167 cast.[13] This defeat seems to indicate that the people were becoming more objective and, perhaps, considerably less emotional.

NOTES TO CHAPTER 11

[1] Anthony Lewis, *Portrait of a Decade* (New York: Random House, 1964), 205.
[2] *Ibid.*
[3] "The Negro Campaign to Win Equal Rights and Opportunities in the U. S.," *Civil Rights, 1960-63* (New York: Facts on File, 1964), 53.
[4] Lewis, *Portrait of a Decade*, 216.   [5] *Ibid.*
[6] Ross Barnett in a television address over WLBT, Jackson, Mississippi, September 13, 1962. The program was also broadcast over radio station WJDX.
[7] *Ibid.*   [8] *Ibid.*   [9] *Ibid.*
[10] McComb (Miss.) *Enterprise-Journal*, September 14, 1962, p. 1.
[11] *Ibid.*
[12] Lillian Smith, *Killers of the Dream* (Garden City, N. Y.: Doubleday & Co., 1949), 182.
[13] McComb (Miss.) *Enterprise-Journal*, August 16, 1967, p. 2.

12 Reign of Terror

THE LAST HALF of 1964 reflected the sentiments, the reactions, the anger, the fear, the frustration, and the bewilderment of citizens in the Deep South when the two incompatible heritages of the South were brought face to face. Although the emotional outbursts which followed were typical of the reaction throughout the region, in order to simplify and condense this narration I am confining it to my own bailiwick, McComb, Mississippi, which is typical of the Deep South as a whole. In the early spring of that year pernicious predictions began to circulate that ahead was a "long, hot summer."

Robert Moses, an honor graduate of Hamilton College and Harvard University who took his M.A. degree in philosophy on a John Hay Whitney Fellowship, became interested in voter registration for black people. After graduating from Harvard, he taught for three years at Horace Mann, one of New York's better private preparatory schools, while he studied for his PhD. He gave up this job in an atmosphere of tranquility and became director of a voter registration project in Mississippi.[1]* He was then shot at, clubbed by police, and bitten by a police dog. While he was in the Pike County jail in Magnolia, seven miles south of McComb, the *Enterprise-Journal* sent my

* Notes appear at end of chapter.

son, a staff member, to interview him. He introduced himself and, extending common courtesy, shook hands with Moses. Because of that simple act, both the reporter and the newspaper were subjected to severe criticism. Unfortunately, at this time an eastern campus newspaper predicted editorially that a blood-bath would accompany the violence of the hot summer and added that the letting of blood would serve a good purpose. An attorney in the county seat aroused even more alarm when he distributed Xerox copies of this editorial to the people of the area.

Wild rumors continued to be circulated, and the air seemed to be charged with electricity. Governor Paul Johnson, Jr., called the legislature into special session.[2] The state highway patrol was increased from 275 to 475 and municipalities deputized special auxiliary police.[3] Asked what would be the state's policy during the predicted "long hot summer," Governor Johnson replied, "The more you talk about the mountain the harder it is to climb." He added, "No one, white, Negro, Chinese, not even my own brother, will be permitted to take the law into his own hands."[4] But obviously, the entire state was preparing for an "invasion." The situation might be compared to the late days of the weakening Roman Empire when the barbarian Goths were expected momentarily from the North to climb or to crumble the walls that protected the empire.

So when a meager force of civil rights workers arrived in town the bombs commenced to explode. A wave of terror swept over the area. There were twenty-five known incidents of arson, beatings, burnings, flogging, and widespread intimidation. Three taverns were burned to the ground. Acts of vandalism were reported. Crosses were burned in public and private places, usually as a warning or to frighten people. In one neighborhood, an organization known as "Help, Inc." was set up to develop a system of alarms, warnings, and instructions as to what the members should do in case of intrusion or attack.[5] The family of Albert Heffner, a local insurance man and the father of "Miss Mississippi" of 1964, was harassed to the point that the Heffners had to leave town. The Heffners had invited some white civil rights workers to their home for a cookout. They moved to Jackson, the capital city, but had to vacate their rented apartment after their identity became known.[6] They finally settled in Washington, D.C.

People became suspicious of one another. There were alarming rumors. One woman who had recently moved into the community from Texas said, "I was at a neighbor's home and listened to so many incendiary remarks that I ran home and wept."

Sixteen churches and Negro residences were dynamited. A Molotov cocktail was hurled against the home of a city official. Household ammonia was tossed in the face of one person. There was a series of harassment arrests.

Many people resented the mass media covering such events and argued that civil rights violence stories should be deleted from the reported news. The newsmen, however, believed that to pursue this course would have been to adopt the policy of darkness which keeps the people of totalitarian countries ignorant and enslaved.

A syndicated columnist, the late Drew Pearson, called me on Sunday morning from New Orleans. He said, "I am in a chartered plane. Can I see you in your office for a few moments?" I agreed. Shortly thereafter a law enforcement officer drove him from the airport to the newspaper office. I invited the officer to remain for the conference between Mr. Pearson and myself. Getting to the point quickly, Pearson said, "I want to know more about the harassment arrests that have been made in McComb." I gave him what information I had. The law enforcement officer commented, "If I had been here they would not have occurred." He explained that he had been out of the city when the arrests were made.

I told Mr. Pearson of my deep concern regarding the tarnished image of our city, state, and region. Others, however, were not so concerned. A few days before, a legislator had been asked about his appraisal of the effects of violence on the state's image. He replied, "To hell with our image." Pearson told me that when the violence had ended he would help to repair the ugly image violence had created. But in the meantime he died.

The day after Pearson's visit I reported in my front page column the statement made by the law officer concerning the harassment arrests—that they would not have occurred had he not been out of the city. I commended him for this responsible position. The following day the officer, in a radio interview, said that I had lied. Inflamed public reaction could well have placed the law enforcement officer under severe pressure and embarrassed him for saying the harassment arrests would not have occurred had he not been away from the community.

Eerie and frightening blasts of exploding dynamite were

often heard in the night. Following a blast, after midnight or at two in the morning, neighbors would gather on the street adjacent to their homes and excitedly speculate on the exact location of the explosion. Estimates of the distance between a given location and a dynamite blast vary from one individual to another. One person may say, "It's just over that hill"; another, "It's two miles from here." McComb by this time had won the title "dynamite capital of the world."

As a newspaper editor, I felt obliged to do whatever I could to apply the force of responsible journalism to the community and state. As the noise of the bombs was heard, we wrote (October 14, 1963): "Negro churches have been burned. Negro homes have been bombed. A Negro store has been dynamited. And with a sense of irresponsibility we have blamed the Negroes for the burnings, the bombing, the dynamiting. This is the sordid story of McComb." [7]

The following excerpt is from an editorial published in the McComb *Enterprise-Journal* on October 15: "Hate begets hate. Hate is unproductive. It destroys those who indulge in it. It tears apart. It crucifies." [8]

On October 16, the following was a part of an editorial in our newspaper: "The difficulty to open-mindedness, an essential to responsible action, is our unwillingness to entertain any idea which threatens the sacred cows grazing upon our own moral, spiritual and intellectual pastures."[9]

The question confronting the newspaper was how to be responsible and effective at the same time. It was easy to be effective and irresponsible. In the years leading to this crisis, our leaders had proved that they could be effective when they advocated such legal maneuvers as interposition, nullification, closing down the public schools, and other approaches to the problem which aroused the hopes of many people but which in the end proved to be empty promises and legal failures.[10]

On October 20, an editorial in the *Enterprise-Journal* stated: "But there is an even more poignant question now: Can community tranquility prevail and progress proceed if we, as advocates of constitutional government, turn our backs upon the Constitution of the United States which is explicit on this point of franchise?" The advice given me in the thirties by Dr. E. Stanley Jones convinced me that America could not tax people without representation and continue to be America.[11]

On October 21, I said editorially: "Elected leadership has led us through the epochal trials of the Southern Manifesto, nullification, interposition, violence, mass resistance, the closing of schools, boycotts, economic pressure. But negation has served only to prove the fruitlessness of such efforts." [12]

Patriotic appeal reproduced below was part of an editorial published on October 22 after the "long hot summer." "Human dignity is as American as the Stars and Stripes or the Declaration of Independence. It is not something which can be bought with a bank account. Yes, the poorest sharecropper, white or Negro, can use it as the foundation upon which to build a successful life." [13]

Obviously, the reverse is true when human dignity is denied any person or any people. I feel this strongly because I have traveled all over the world—into about eighty countries—and I have been impressed with how many people covet the idea of living in America, "the land of the free and the home of the brave." I know that this American concept must prevail if America is to be perpetuated.

This editorial appeal was published on October 23: "Too often we complain about the centralization of power in Washington. Yet, we overlook the fact that the surest way to promote centralization is to irresponsibly ignore and neglect problems at the local level." [14] The following editorial suggestion to clergymen in the McComb area is an excerpt from a full-sized editorial: "Our ministers in the McComb area can help tremendously in restoring responsible behavior. The mere mention of community responsibility in the pulpit would emphasize it."

One church in town had what it called the "nigger committee," a body of men who stood in the vestibule of the church to intercept any black person, and to request courteously that he or she not come into the sanctuary. If the unwelcome visitor persisted, he was to be warned that the police would be called to arrest him.

It would seem that a terrified people would welcome an effort to restore order and tranquility. But it must be remembered that these people were disturbed, confused, and frightened. History was bearing down upon them. Some were racists. Others were conformists—and conformity prevailed.

Because of the newspaper's efforts to provide the community with responsible journalism, rifle fire was directed at the newspaper office. The plate glass windows were smashed. A stink bomb was thrown into the circulation department. Harassment telephone calls and hostile anonymous letters were received. A cross was burned in front of the newspaper office. Another cross was burned on the lawn of my residence on the night of the day my mother died. I must admit that a man did call on me to say apologetically, "We would not have burned that cross in front of your home had we known of your mother's death." A Molotov cocktail was thrown against a window in the home of managing editor, Charles Dunagin.

On October 26, 1964, we ran an editorial earnestly pleading for citizens to join in a responsible effort to return our city to normalcy. A careful scrutiny of this editorial, which follows, reveals the extreme difficulty involved in overcoming conformity.[15]

> The time is here to move the McComb community into a new era of responsibility.
>
> In the editorial published in the *Enterprise-Journal* we have pointed realistically to the consistent failures of negation. A positive program is our only means of restoring a sense of responsibility in McComb.
>
> The question is: Who in our community can make a positive program a reality?
>
> The average individual expresses apprehension. Many of our people are afraid. Generally our people are frustrated.
>
> The answer can be found in community action. With this in mind we appeal to individuals in several categories of our civic, business, industrial and domestic life. Below we list the categories to which this appeal is directed.
>
> ### BANKERS
>
> The bankers in the McComb area—board chairmen,

presidents, cashiers, tellers—rank high in responsibility. Is it reasonable to believe that there can be a responsible meeting of minds in the area of banking which could aid in helping to develop a sound way out of our conflicts?

MERCHANTS

This appeal is made to our responsible merchants. In a sense most businesses are merchandising firms. Too many of us have been too timid, fearful that any expression of positive opinion might result in boycotts, harassment and intimidation.

Current frustrations are proving injurious to business generally. There are far too many vacant buildings in McComb. Many Negro people, fearful of the tension or resentful of things which have happened, are avoiding our retail establishments. Responsible merchants can help by discussing a positive program even if it is limited to merchants, themselves.

LAWYERS

Our attorneys are in an enviable position to render constructive aid in helping to restore normalcy. They know the law. They are by profession sworn to uphold the law. They are dedicated to it.

INDUSTRIAL WORKERS

Mechanics and technicians love their children as all of us do. They comprehend the need of responsible community action, knowing this is essential to the best interests of our children, our homes, and our future. Our industrial workers can help. Their cooperation is solicited.

SCHOOL TEACHERS

Where can a more dedicated group of people be found outside the Christian ministry itself? They know that responsible community goals, goals within the law, must be upheld in the best interest of our young people. The McComb region can rely upon our school teachers in helping to steer us into an era of responsible thinking.

RAILROADMEN

The McComb area has grown up with the helpful influence of people in the realm of transportation. In this crisis of McComb, when people indicate a fear to express themselves responsibly, we believe that engineers, conductors, trainmen, firemen, maintenance men, clerks and others, recognize the need of meeting our critical problems steadfastly. Our railroad people for the most part are local homeowners. Their influence is solicited in this needed drive for community responsibility.

HOUSEWIVES

Amazing progress can be achieved if the housewives of the area take up the challenge and become crusaders for community responsibility in the interest of our children.

MINISTERS

Our ministers in the McComb area can help tremendously in restoring responsible behavior. The mere mentioning of community responsibility in the pulpits would emphasize it. The endorsement of the concept of the dignity of the individual could be a pulpit contribution to responsible action. Christian idealism must become embedded in the conscience of each of us.

Baptists, Methodists, Presbyterians, Catholics, Episcopalians, Lutherans, Nazarenes, Disciples of Christ—all of our Christian denominations represented in the McComb area—have an obligation. Silence may be golden but not where there exists the imperative need of responsible articulation.

REIGN OF TERROR

The ugly national image of the McComb area is hurting far more than many of us know.

Unless our people take up the suggested crusade for responsibility it can be expected that some of our business houses will close down, more buildings will be vacated, property values will diminish and industry will pass us by.

Instead of moving from one irresponsible failure to another we must adopt a responsible, positive program. In so doing we will discover that we can and will triumph over the fears and tension which frustrate us.

We must halt the deterioration of the McComb community. But many must be willing to help if we are to hope for an early era of community responsibility.

The above editorial pleaded, begged, implored in an effort to halt the divorce proceedings the McComb community was waging against reality. It tried to encourage an escape from negativism, a reach for positive action. Soon thereafter a spark of hope was ignited.

Then on October 26, the following question was asked: "Our people are frightened. Frightened people cannot attain progress. Nor can a frightened people re-establish community peace and tranquility. Of whom and of what are we afraid?"

On October 27, the newspaper warned: "The days ahead are not nearly so dark as they appear—and for one reason. Our people will come to the realization of the need of positive, responsible thinking—and supply it. This is the reason for our faith in our home town and our area."

Then it became known that, just a few weeks before, the community had been threatened with martial law. The report was not hearsay. Roughly one thousand soldiers were readied to be sent to McComb—60 percent white, 40 percent black. The thought of martial law was discomforting to the more serious-minded citizens of the community.

On October 30, the newspaper said: "Responsible men must recognize there is an economic aspect to law and order. Property values are tied to them. And this we know: Responsible men can correct the wrongs and the weakness which now exist in this area of public service."

It was a cloudy day, but somehow the sun commenced to break through the dark clouds above.

NOTES TO CHAPTER 12

[1] John Fischer, "A Small Band of Practical Heroes," *Harper's Magazine*, CCXXVII (October, 1963), 16.
[2] Governor's Proclamation, June 11, 1964.
[3] Mississippi House of Representatives, regular session, 1964, House Bill 564.
[4] Conversation with author, Jackson, Mississippi, April 20, 1964.
[5] Hodding Carter, *So The Heffners Left McComb* (Garden City, N. Y.: Doubleday & Co., 1965), 67.
[6] *Ibid.*, 88.
[7] McComb (Miss.) *Enterprise-Journal*, October 14, 1964, p. 2.
[8] *Ibid.*, October 15, 1964, p. 2. [9] *Ibid.*, October 16, 1964, p. 2.
[10] *Ibid.*, October 19, 1964, p. 2. [11] *Ibid.*, October 20, 1964, p. 2.
[12] *Ibid.*, October 21, 1964, p. 2. [13] *Ibid.*, October 22, 1964, p. 2.
[14] *Ibid.*, October 23, 1964, p. 2. [15] *Ibid.*, October 26, 1964, p. 2.

13 The Sheriff's Request

THE LATE SHERIFF R. R. Warren of Pike County, Mississippi, was a conscientious and responsible law enforcement officer. On a Friday morning in the fall of 1964 he walked into the newspaper office.

"If I had some money to offer as rewards or with which to buy information I could solve these dynamiting cases." he said.

"How much do you need?" he was asked.

"$2,500," was the response.

A front page editorial appeared in the newspaper that afternoon making known the sheriff's request and urging people to subscribe the requested money. Within a few hours four local businessmen, a merchant, an insurance man, an attorney, and an editor met and agreed to attempt to raise the money.

The following morning, a stranger walked into the newspaper office and announced he was from Washington and had a check to provide money to be used by the sheriff to buy information or to be offered as rewards.

Although the offer appeared genuine enough, the visitor was told that it might be a mistake to accept it. "Why?" he asked. The reply was: "If people in McComb are willing to subscribe this money it will be evidence of restored confidence. The very knowledge about town that the sheriff's request has been met would help restore law and order and prove to the entire community that concerned people at last have become weary with violence and are willing to do something about it." The man from Washington quickly caught the idea and agreed to wait and give the committee time to see how much money it could raise.

On Sunday afternoon three members of the committee met in a car parked on a residential street. The committee decided to increase its goal from the requested $2,500 to $5,000. No one other than the three men in the car could have heard the conversation. No cars were parked nearby. The only time the figure "$5,000" was mentioned outside the car was when one committeeman telephoned the fourth one that the goal had been changed to $5,000.

That night one committee member received an anonymous telephone call. The anonymous caller tried to dissuade the committeeman from raising the $5,000 as planned. The obvious conclusion was that the telephones of at least some members of the committee had been tapped.

Within forty-eight hours the committee had the $5,000 in hand. Some people donated cash. Some paid by check.

The committee decided to deliver the money to the sheriff with the understanding that he could use it as he deemed wise. There was one stipulation. If he still had any funds on hand at the end of twenty-four months the balance was to be returned to the committeemen for pro rata refunds to the original donors.

Within several weeks, the sheriff, with the effective support of the Federal Bureau of Investigation and the state Highway Patrol had located the meeting place of the dyna-

THE SHERIFF'S REQUEST

miters. There was a stake-out. When a number of participants were gathered in this home, officers executed a raid, made arrests, and confiscated a cache of weapons. The objects found by the law enforcement officers included high-powered rifles, KKK membership cards, and records of guns ordered by individuals, all of which were later used as evidence in the courts. After these arrests were made, thousands of people breathed sighs of relief. It had been said that an overt act on the part of black people could have possibly ended with mass bloodletting. The unknown identity of the dynamiters had added mystery to the situation during the period of dynamiting and had increased the tension of an already extremely tense situation.

The odd thing about the dynamiters, mostly young men, was that they had heard so much talk concerning preparation for an "invasion" and had witnessed a legislature which actually was preparing to cope with an "invasion," as evidenced, for example, by the doubling of the state highway patrol, that they probably regarded themselves as patriots. They acted as if they were trying to protect the homes and the lives of their people.

Circuit Judge W. H. Watkins, Jr., presided over the trials of nine duly indicted individuals who were brought into the court room. The judge told them they were involved in sedition, a crime very close to treason. He lectured the nine men sternly, then issued unprecedented sentences. Two of the men received three five-year penitentiary sentences to run concurrently, four men were to serve five-year penitentiary sentences, and the other three were sentenced to six months in the county jail and fined five hundred dollars each.

The judge then shocked the nation and came under severe criticism when he suspended the sentences and placed the men on probation. When the conditions of the judge's suspension of sentences were announced many people wondered whether he had proved himself to be a wise judge. Judge Watkins announced that these sentences required that the men must not only not break the law, but if another wave of racial violence occurred their probations could be revoked whether or not the defendants in these cases were participants in the violence. Furthermore, they could have no firearms, no live ammunition, and no dynamite or other combustibles in their homes or in their possession.

Then questions were asked: had the judge shown compassion to these individuals or was he attempting to bring an end to the dynamiting and the bombing? Was he ignoring the concept of criminal punishment? Was he attempting to return the community to a state of peace and tranquility? Or was he from a pragmatic viewpoint restraining every person in the county?

From the standpoint of practicability, Judge Watkins had indicted all citizens of the county. He said, when passing sentence, "If violence is renewed, you can be picked up by the sheriff and incarcerated in the state penitentiary." It was generally believed that the dynamiters had had the support of some leading citizens in the community. Despite the criticism, which came largely from other states, the

THE SHERIFF'S REQUEST

dynamiting, the violence, and the bombing of homes and churches came to a sudden halt.

Membership of the committee which raised the five thousand dollars for the sheriff was increased to eight, then to ten, then to twenty. From time to time it was further enlarged. A mass meeting of the townspeople was held at the city hall for the purpose of forming an agreement by which responsible community life could be restored and the people, white and black, given a new freedom—freedom from hysteria.

The following statement of principles was drawn up and presented to the gathered crowd:

> The great majority of our citizens believe in law and order and are against violence of any kind. In spite of this, acts of terrorism have been committed numerous times against citizens both Negro and white.
> We believe the time has come for responsible people to speak out for what is right and against what is wrong. For too long we have let the extremists on both sides bring our community close to chaos.
> There is only one responsible stance we can take, and that is for equal treatment under the law for all citizens regardless of race, creed, position or wealth; for making our protests within the framework of the law; and for obeying the laws of the land regardless of our personal feelings. Certain of these laws may be contrary to our traditions, customs or beliefs, but as God-fearing men and women, and as citizens of these United States, we see no other honorable course to follow.
> To these ends and for the purpose of restoring peace,

tranquility and progress to our area, we respectfully urge the following:

1) Order and respect for law must be re-established and maintained.

    a) Law officers should make only lawful arrests. Harassment arrests, no matter what the provocation, are not consonant with impartiality of the law.

    b) To insure the confidence of the people in their officials, we insist that no man is entitled to serve in a public office, elective or appointive, who is a member of any organization declared to be subversive by the Senate Internal Security Sub-Committee or the United States Army, Navy or Air Force, or to take any obligation upon himself in conflict with his oath of office.

2) Economic threats and sanctions against people of both races must be ended. They only bring harm to both races.

3) We urge citizens of both races to re-establish avenues of communication and understanding. In addition, it is urged that the Negro leadership cooperate with local officials.

4) We urge widest possible use of our citizenship in the selection of juries. We further urge that men called for jury duty not be excused except for the most compelling reasons.

5) We urge our fellow citizens to take a greater interest in public affairs, in the selection of candidates, and in the support and/or constructive criticism of Public Servants.

6) We urge all of our people to approach the future with a renewed dedication and to reflect an attitude of optimism about our county.

We, the undersigned, have read and hereby subscribe to and support the principles and purposes herein set forth.

THE SHERIFF'S REQUEST

This statement of principles was signed by 650 citizens and published with the signers' names as a full-page advertisement in the local daily newspaper. Other citizens were invited to sign the document.[1*]

Immediately the atmosphere, long charged as with electricity, cleared. Tension was lessened. The citizenry had finally evinced responsible concern.

Five black leaders of the community called at the newspaper and expressed appreciation for the action taken by the white people. The leader of the group commented to the editor, "We want to make a conciliatory statement and we want you to write it for us." The editor suggested the black people themselves should prepare the statement and offered to publish it without cost.

The following day the black committee returned with its statement which expressed both agreement and gratitude. Instead of carrying individuals' signatures, it was signed on behalf of twelve recognized black organizations. The fact that it was sponsored by twelve black organizations cleared the way for the creation of a bi-racial committee.

After all, how do you go about naming the black members of a bi-racial committee? Intimidated blacks are often, and rightfully, afraid to venture. If they accept an invitation from whites to serve, they may be called "Uncle Toms" by members of their own race. It so happened that the permanent committee of "Citizens for Progress" consisted of twelve whites. To create a bi-racial committee, it was agreed that the president of each black organization

* Notes appear at end of chapter.

name one member of his group to serve on a twenty-four man bi-racial committee—twelve blacks and twelve whites. At the first meeting of the committee, an elderly Negro minister suggested that everyone join hands and sing "Amazing Grace."

NOTES TO CHAPTER 13

[1] McComb (Miss.) *Enterprise-Journal*, November 18, 1964.

14 The Road to Damascus

EIGHT YEARS AFTER "the long hot summer of 1964," the Deep South people, like Saul of Tarsus, have walked along "the road to Damascus." Colossal changes have come to pass in a short time. Self-examination by thousands of Deep South folk will reveal that this superlative, *colossal,* as used here, is by no means an exaggeration.

A miracle was performed when Saul of Tarsus became the time-honored and revered Saint Paul. What has recently happened in the Deep South can truthfully be described as something very close to a miracle, if not, in truth, a miracle itself.

Ten lears ago a Negro man took a seat at a Woolworth's counter and ordered a hamburger and a cold drink. He was immediately shampooed with mustard and catsup. Six years ago in the South had he sat at a restaurant table everyone would have stared at him askance. Today no one expresses surprise when a black man or his family seeks public accommodations in any place of business.

In the beginning, changes were accomplished as the result of the force of law or the threat of losing federal grants. It would be untrue to say that federal funds and federal force are no longer a factor in the change. But it must also be said that much of the new motivation of whites stems from the will of the people to respect and apply that American concept which upholds justice and the dignity of the individual.

The philosophy of backwardness—with its hostility to change, its demand for conformity, its unyielding provincialism, its feeling of always being on the defensive, a philosophy which history for more than a hundred years has burned into the hearts and minds and souls of men like a hot branding iron pressed against the side or shoulder of a struggling steer—has in the thinking of many southerners yielded to the broader concepts of the American heritage.

A few years ago, whites physically resisted the registration of blacks to vote. Today, following the acceptance of the statement of principles at the mass meeting a new spiritual force is at work. Black voters freely participate in elections. They are among the workers at the polls. White candidates solicit black voters' support and black voters support both white and black candidates. A black man said to me, "Don't overlook the fact that we want good government, too, and we know that the place to find it is at the polls. So we try to determine which candidate can better serve the cause of good government."

Norwood Jones, an executive with the Kellwood Company, declared in 1969, "I don't know what we would have done had it not been for the new supply of black labor which has enabled us to meet the demands for expansion." Blacks are employed in McComb banks, in the sheriff's office, in the stores, and offices, and in industries. The availability of better jobs for blacks has aided business rather than handicapped it. Anyone acquainted with business in the town once called the "dynamite capital of the world" will agree that it is brisk. Such indicators as the retail sales tax reveal business now to be at an unprecedented high.

Participation in all areas of community activity has helped to provide a higher quality of life for our black people. By abandoning their long-held fears and suspicions, whites, too, are sharing a better quality of life. The subject of combatting harmful drugs was discussed at a dinner served in the substory of the J. J. White Memorial Presbyterian Church. Blacks and whites participated in the meeting. This was done with a normal approach because everyone knows that drugs constitute a threat to children of both white and black parents.

In the schools children are adjusting to a national challenge. At Southwest General Hospital a "pink lady," the name given to volunteer workers, walked into the room of a black patient. The patient told the pink lady, "I am a teacher. I teach mathematics to the more advanced pupils." When questioned further, she showed the pink lady messages and gifts she had received from some of her white pupils. The school's football team, track team, basketball teams, and school band include both white and black pupils. So do the squad of cheerleaders, the choral group, and the classes. No one would be so foolish as to say that problems have not arisen, but the people are willing to seek solutions to these problems. The effort is being made to find solutions; for only solutions, not violence, can remove frustration.

The police department no longer makes harassment arrests. There is no such thing in the area as "police brutality." Both races are represented in the police department. One school patron said, "I didn't realize how wrong I was when I said 'our state.' I used to consider the state as a state for whites only." There is now black participation in the McComb area. Blacks are represented on the school board, the hospital board, the housing board, the urban renewal board, and the board of directors of the Chamber of Commerce. They participate in the Azalea Parade, the Christmas Parade, and the Concert Association.

At first the blending of interests stemmed from various forms of force. But the greatest stimulus for a better day has come from recognition by whites of what is fair and right, legal and logical. This spirit is regional.

A truth which could well have surprised many people is that the realm of politics has not gotten worse as a result of enfranchising the Negro people. Conversely, politics has improved. The reason is simple. No longer can irresponsible candidates use the black man as a political "whipping boy" to arouse emotional fervor. Responsible candidates now can emphasize the real issues of the hour. This approach was impractical when blacks were denied full citizenship.

These are not isolated examples of a new day dawning. Across the Deep South—in Georgia and Alabama, in South Carolina and Arkansas, in Mississippi and Louisiana—the cottonpatch philosophy is yielding to the forces of enlightenment. A thousand Deep South communities can make this testimony. And they boast of it.

What has happened in this region in recent years must be accepted as the achievement of a new enlightenment. It also provides a new freedom for white people who were tied to a pattern of militant conformity. Conformity, unrestrained and uninhibited, becomes a form of slavery. Conformity becomes a master. On numerous occasions throughout the years I have had good men whisper to me at times of heated debates, "You are right but don't mention my name." Escape from this master means a new freedom for the white people who were enslaved by it.

No Utopia exists. But the road traveled today is in the direction of government by law as contrasted with government by men.

In this effort to become free from violence and to find peace and tranquility, the black people have been exceedingly patient and cooperative. A white woman said recently of the black people, "We must be patient with them because they have been patient with us for a long, long time."

People outside the Deep South should recognize this epochal change. They should not err by thinking of yesterday and calling it today. They may continue to think of the Deep South that was and not grasp the reality of the Deep South that is. There is a human tendency to think and live in the past. Thus it is difficult for people to recognize the new viewpoints and new patterns which other persons have accepted.

An attractive blonde reporter from a Stockholm daily newspaper called at the *Enterprise-Journal* office several years after the explosions which gave my town the title of "the dynamite capital of the world." She was preparing an article for her Swedish newspaper and asked me if I would drive her to the ruins of the dynamited churches for photographs."

I replied, "Those churches were bombed six years ago. They have been rebuilt. Our own people contributed along with others to rebuild them and the new buildings are more attractive than the churches which they replaced."

When tourists of the East visit western states they do not look for the modern triumphs of industry and commerce. They want to visit deserted ghost towns and abandoned gold mines or the place where Jesse James was shot while hanging a picture on a wall. When they come South they want to see black women wearing red and white polka dot bandanas while picking cotton in the field—or dynamited churches in McComb. This is the yesterday we want to forget.

Over and over again for three quarters of a century, Southern leaders have spoken of the "New" South. As early as December, 1886, Henry Grady, editor of the Atlanta *Constitution*, spoke to the New England Club of New York City. His subject was, "The New South." At a time when people, North and South, were eager for the culmination of the spirit of the Civil War, which had taken a death toll of 498,432 Americans—364,511 Union soldiers, and 133,921 Confederates—his forensic appeal fell on friendly ears. He said that the Old South, the South of slavery, was dead; that the New South was born.

But Henry Grady, despite his eloquence, his dedication, and his will to see old hatreds die, was wrong. The New South had not arrived in 1886. The Old South, its prejudices glamorized under the more polite term of "southern traditions," was by no means dead. War and defeat had changed the U. S. Constitution, but old traditions—to which the Old South was irrevocably bound—were still the living sentiment of the people. Before the New South could be born a transformation had to come to pass.

The New South was not here in 1886. Nor was it here in 1896, nor in 1906, nor in 1926. The spirit of the Old South still endured in 1956. Despite the traumatic experiences associated with the Civil War the South, even in 1956, did not admit that the war had been an historic mistake and a source of needless catastrophe. The spirit of slavery still prevailed. The New South could not emerge triumphant, even at that late hour in history, because the people of the Deep South were trapped by a formula, a set of rules, an historical dogma, a provincial code. Tenets advanced as authoritative, but which the rest of the nation would not accept, tied the South to the dead centuries of the past. The Old South even persisted in 1964, the year of the "long hot summer."

This is the reason that the changes in the Deep South in recent years represent something resembling a miracle. The New South today is coming alive because southern people at long last are manifesting a willingness to come face to face with reality. Comparatively few Americans across the nation are aware of this historic breakthrough. Fewer still recognize the reason for this spectacular achievement.

The difference between the Old South and the New South is primarily a difference in the attitudes of the people. The willingness of some, the reluctance of others, to abandon concepts which conflict with the Constitution of our country—these attitudes mark the division and are the reason for the delay in the fruition of a New South. What has happened to create this New South is an unknown factor to many Americans today. But today a New South is in the process of being born. The evidence of it can be seen in the new thinking and feeling of the people.

This is important to both whites and blacks in the South: important to blacks because the transformation was necessary to uproot the historic remnants of slavery; important to whites because freedom was thwarted for all people so long as the evils of slavery were not frowned upon; important to all people of the region because the New South could not gloriously unfold and abundantly achieve the potential of its destiny until the transition between the New and the Old South had been fulfilled.

The two faces of Janus have haunted the Deep South. But there is evidence suggesting the faces may blend into one. Out of the agony and trauma of the past, lessons have been etched into the souls of men. If we continue on the "road to Damascus," the two faces may become synchronized and both can face in one direction—the direction of an inevitably brilliant and rewarding future with progress the world well may describe as spectacular. By no means have all Deep South problems been solved. The economic gap between this region and the rest of the nation is still present. But a new spirit has been born. This spirit is part of the saga of Deep South change.

Don't scorn the Deep South. A miracle has come to pass—and the destiny of the South—perhaps even of all America—is irrevocably linked together by it.

Index

Adams, John Quincy, 9
Africa, 77, 78, 111
Agricultural Adjustment Administration, 73
Alabama, 12, 13, 49, 50, 54, 57, 87, 90, 92, 94, 96, 98, 101
Alcorn A&M College, 70
Alsop, Joseph, 101
Alsop, Stewart, 101
American Revolution, 90
Amite County, Miss., 25, 35, 36, 39, 40
Atlanta *Constitution*, 15, 156

"Back-to-Africa" movement, 77–78
Bailey, Tom, 69
Barkley, Alben, 76, 82, 93
Barnett, Ross: bars Meredith from Ole Miss, 121–30 *passim*
Barr, John U., 92
Bickham, Frank, 25–26
Bickham, Maria, 25–26
Bickham, Oliver, 27
Bickham, Sis, 25–28
Bilbo, Theodore G.: accused of bribery, 59–60, 62; described by W. A. Percy, 61; his "dream house," 67–68, 81, 84; elected to state office, 56, 62, 63; his feud with Sullens, 55, 58, 63, 74; fires faculty members, 65–67; and state debt, 69; as U.S. senator, 75–84; mentioned, 48–51, 53, 95, 126. *See also* "Back-to-Africa" movement; Long, Huey P.

Black, Hugo L., 122
Bond, W. F. 83
Bonner, J. M. 82
Boston Tea Party, 32, 90
Boulton, Matthew, 7
Bradley, Omar, 114
Brady, Tom, 92
Brewer, Earl, 62–63
Brooklyn *Eagle*, 47
Busby, Dick, 114

Cameron, Ben F., 122
Campaign Investigating Committee, 80
Cannon, Joe, 50
Cash, W. J., 8, 52
Cassidy, Jim, 63
Castleman, Steve, 62–63
Cattle: and tick eradication, 34–42
Chicago *Tribune*, 47
Churchill, Winston, 124
"Citizens for Progress," 149–50
Civil rights: campaign for, 78, 91, 94, 95, 99, 100, 123, 151; and violence, 132–42 *passim*, 143–50
Civil War, the, 8, 156–57
Cohn, David, 9
Congressional Record, the, 78
Conner, Mike, 69, 73
Cornwallis, Charles, 1st Marquis, 32
Cotton: described by Henry Grady, 15–16, 156; related to "philosophy of backwardness," 4–5, 9–10, 14, 16, 17, 23, 53, 62, 87, 88, 105, 108, 109, 110, 111, 120,

159

INDEX

129, 152; its rivalry with wool, 11–12; mentioned, 45, 51–52
Crisler, H. H., 69–70
Critz, Hugh, 66

Daughters of the American Revolution, 68
Davis, Jefferson, 44, 130
Davis, Jimmie, 122
Declaration of Independence, 32, 124, 125, 136
Democratic party, 76, 87, 89, 94, 95, 98, 99, 102, 105
Dewey, Tom, 98
"Dilemma in Mississippi": *See Life*
Divinity, Howard, 19–23
Dixon, Frank, 99
Dowsing, Frank, vii
Dunagin, Charles, 138

Easom, Percy, 31
Ebony. See Rowan, Carl
Edwards, R. E., 24–25
Ellis, Hardy, 96
Emmerich, J. Oliver: his editorials, 40–41, 89, 105, 135–42, 143–44; interviewed in *Ebony*, 109–10; mentioned, 104, 116
England: textiles in, 7, 10–12

Fair Employment Practices Act, 78–79
Faser, John Minor, 96
Faubus, Orval, 122
Ferguson, Jim, 47–48
Ferguson, Miriam Wallace, 47–48
Foreman, Rodney, 35
Franklin, Benjamin, 33
"Freedom riders," 128
Furbay, John, 110–11

Garibaldi, Giuseppe, 124
Gatlin, "Uncle John," 40
George III, 32, 90
Gibbs, W. D., 61–62
Gibson, Meredith, 92
Gibson, Merritt, 99

Godwin, George, 99
Goodman, Bob, 92
Gore, Weaver, 96
Go South to Sorrow. See Rowan, Carl
"Go to Jail First," 125
Grady, Henry: on cotton, 15–16, 156
Green, A. Wigfall, 63, 81
Green, Widow Nathanael, 6

Harris, Leon, 92
Harrison, Pat, 73–74, 76–77
Harvey, Bob, 23–25
Heffner, Albert, 133
Heflin, Tom, 49, 50, 51, 53, 87
Henry, Hi, 58
Henry, Pat, 63
Henry, Patrick, 32, 33, 122, 124
Hindus, 10, 12
Hobbs, G. A., 63
Holmes, Edwin R., 63–64, 76–77
Hudson, John B., 65
Humphrey, Hubert, 95
Hutson, Higdon, 35–36

Indus Valley, 6
Issaquena County, Miss., 59

Jackson, Miss.: newspapers in, 58, 60–61, 84, 107; mentioned, x, 29, 57, 59, 80, 92, 99, 106, 107, 126, 133
Jackson, "Stonewall," 20
Janus: in Roman mythology, vii, 3; and cotton, 6, 7, 8, 9, 13, 15, 16, 119, 120, 158
Jefferson, Thomas, 33
Johnson, Paul, Jr., 132
Joint Committee on Contingent Funds, 59
Jones, E. Stanley, 29–33 *passim*, 89–90, 136
Jones, Norwood, 152
Jones, Sam, 101
Juniper Grove, Miss., 55, 67, 83
Keesler Air Field, 81

160

INDEX

"King Cotton," vii, 3, 8, 10
Kirkland, J. H., 66
Kirwan, Albert D., 59
Klotz, S. Paul, 104
Kramer, X. A., 112

Laney, Ben, 92, 93, 95
Lanim, Howard, 97
Lanterns on the Levee. See Percy, William Alexander
Lee, Robert E., 19, 20, 44, 100, 101
Lehman, Milton, 73
Liberty, Miss.: *Southern Herald* in, 39; mentioned, 35
Life, 79, 97, 115–16
Lincoln, Abraham, 45, 124
Long, Huey P., 48–51, 75–76, 83, 87
Louisiana: cattle tick in, 39–42; and Long, 48–49, 75–76, 87; mentioned, 90, 92, 100, 101, 121, 122
Lynchings, 78, 79, 88, 90–91

McClellan, John, 95
McComb *Enterprise-Journal*: and circulation boycott, 127–28; takes stand on civil rights, 135–42, 143–44; mentioned, 27, 131–32, 155
McComb, Miss., vii, 19, 24, 41, 109, 110, 113, 114, 115, 131, 133–42, 143–50 *passim*, 154, 156. *See also* McComb *Enterprise-Journal*
McIntosh, Frank, 23
McLaurin, Anselm J., 58
Marshall, Thurgood, 108–109
May, Walter Dent, 102
Mead, James, 80–81
Memphis, Tenn., 56
Meredith, James, 121–22
Michie, Allen, 48–49
Millsaps College, 29
Mind of the South, The: *See* Cash, W. J.
Minneapolis *Star-Tribune*, 109
Minor, Wilson, 102, 106

Mississippi:
 Agricultural Extension Service, 4
 Delta, 46, 56–57, 58, 62
 Department of Agriculture and Commerce, 67
 Institutions of Higher Learning, 69
 Press Association, 65
 River, 14, 39, 48
 State Department of Education, 31
 State University, vii, 4
 University of, 66, 96, 121, 126
Missouri, University of, 4
Mize, Sidney C., 121
Monroe, James, 9
Moody, Dan, 94
Moses, Robert, 131–32
Murphree, Dennis, 21
Murray, Bill, 51
Murrow, Edward R., 109

Nash, Mrs. Sidney, vii
Natchez *Democrat*, 47
National Association for the Advancement of Colored People, 108
National Democratic Party Convention (1948), 87, 92
Negroes: and armed services, 78, 80; and civil rights, 131–42 *passim*, 143–50; and demagogues, 46, 49, 52–53, 77–78; and education, 31, 70, 110, 112–13, 153; and employment, 88, 114, 152; hospitals for, 113–14; and journalism, 116–18; and Truman, 78; and voting, 29–33, 78, 80, 152, 154; mentioned, 47, 57, 115, 151. *See also Life*
New Orleans, La.: *Times-Picayune* in, 102, 106; mentioned, 21, 24, 76, 82, 115, 133
New Republic. *See* Hudson, John B.
New York, N. Y.: *Times* in, 47,

161

INDEX

122; mentioned, 79, 80, 93, 131, 156
Numa Pompilius, 3

O'Daniel, W. Lee, 49, 51
"Ole Miss." *See* Mississippi: University of
Oxford, Miss., 64, 76–77

Pakistan, 6
Patton, George, 99
Pearl River County, Miss., 40, 55, 56
Pearson, Drew, 133–34
Percy, Leroy, 58–61
Percy, William Alexander, 61
Perez, Leander, 92
Peterson, Jim, 92
Philadelphia Convention. *See* National Democratic Party Convention (1948)
Poplarville, Miss., 68, 84
Populism, 50, 51, 52, 53
Port Gibson (Miss.) *Reveille*, 70
Prentiss, Sargent S., 16–17

Quin, Oliver B., 27

Ramsey, E. H., 92
Reconstruction, 52, 88, 92
Republican party, 98
Revolt of the Rednecks. See Kirwan, Albert D.
Rhylick, Frank, 48–49
Roosevelt, Eleanor, 77
Rowan, Arch, 92
Rowan, Carl, 109–10
Rushton, Marion, 92
Russ, Edward, vii
Russell, Lee, 63–64, 77
Russell, Richard, 98

Sanders, Dick, 107
Saturday Evening Post. See Lehman, Milton
Senate War Investigating Committee, 80–81

Senate Works Relief Bill, 77
Shakespeare, William, 83
Sigma Delta Chi, 106–107
Sillers, Walter, 92, 98, 99
Sitton, Claude, 122
Slavery, 9–10, 13–15, 45, 108, 109, 119, 157, 158
Smith, Frank, 124
Smith, Gerald K., 80
Smith County, Miss., 36
South Carolina, 49, 54, 91, 92, 93, 94, 98, 100, 101, 121
Southern Association of Colleges and Secondary Schools, 66
Southern Methodist University, 108
Southwest Mississippi Junior College, vii
States' rights campaign (1948), 87, 89, 90, 91–102
Stephens, Hubert, 74, 75
"Stormy Petrel." *See* Bilbo, Theodore G.
Stratton, A. G., 39
Stroupe, Phil, 107
Sullens, Frederick, 55, 57–58, 60, 63, 64, 74, 84
Summit, Miss., 36

Taft, Robert, 79–80, 83
Talmadge, Eugene, 50, 51
Taylor, Glenn, 82
Texas: cattle tick in, 34; mentioned, 47–48, 90, 92, 94, 128, 133
The Man Bilbo. See Green, A. Wigfall
Thurmond, John, 100
Thurmond, George Washington, 100–101
Thurmond, Strom, 91, 92, 100
Tillman, "Pitchfork" Ben, 49, 50, 54
Time, 41
Travis County, Texas, 47
Truman, Harry: his "four-point program," 88, 95; wins nomination, 98; mentioned, 78–79, 88, 91–92, 93, 99, 101–102

INDEX

Tuck, William, 92

Upchurch, Frank, 92
United Daughters of the
  Confederacy, 67–68
United States:
  Congress, 50, 95
  Constitution, 45, 94, 124, 136, 157
  Information Agency, 109
  Senate, 75, 76, 79, 82, 88, 95
  Supreme Court, 104, 108, 109,
    122, 127

Valley Hill, 56
Vanderbilt University, 66
Vardaman, James K., 45–47, 51,
  54, 58–59, 62
Vaughan, George, 93–94
Veterans Administration, 113–14
Vicksburg, Miss., 56
Virginia Assembly, 9, 122

Wallace, Henry, 98
War Between the States, 9, 101, 122
Warren, George, 92
Warren, R. R., 143
Washington, Booker T., 91
Washington, D. C., 49, 73–76, 79,
  82, 84, 94, 112, 113, 114, 133,
  143, 144
Washington, George, 6, 33, 81, 100
Washington County, Miss., 47, 62
Watkins, W. H., Jr., 145–46
Watson, Thomas E., 50
White, Hugh, 96
White House, the, 49
White supremacy, 45, 50, 57
Whitfield, Henry, 64, 65
Whitney, Eli, 6, 7, 8
Wilkins, Roy, 108
Williams, Oliver, 27
Wright, Fielding, 89, 92, 98, 100
Wright, Wally, 99